A Way with Words

Resource Pack 1

- ◆ Vocabulary activities
- ◆ Lower intermediate to intermediate

Stuart Redman, Robert Ellis
with Brigit Viney

Advisory editor: Michael McCarthy

CAMBRIDGE
UNIVERSITY PRESS

PUBLISHED BY THE PRESS SYNDICATE OF THE UNIVERSITY OF CAMBRIDGE

The Pitt Building, Trumpington Street, Cambridge, United Kingdom

CAMBRIDGE UNIVERSITY PRESS

The Edinburgh Building, Cambridge CB2 2RU, UK   http://www.cup.cam.ac.uk

40 West 20th Street, New York, NY 10011–4211, USA   http://www.cup.org

10 Stamford Road, Oakleigh, Melbourne 3166, Australia

Ruiz de Alarcón 13, 28014 Madrid, Spain

First published 1996
Fourth printing 2000

Printed in the United Kingdom at the University Press, Cambridge

A catalogue record for this book is available from the British Library

ISBN 0 521 47775 1   Resource book
ISBN 0 521 47776 X   Cassette

Contents

Introduction

A Way with Words Resource Pack 1 is a new resource book for teachers containing photocopiable materials for use in the classroom. The activities in the pack come from the original *A Way with Words*, Books 1 and 2, although some of the listening passages have been rerecorded, and in a limited number of exercises new activities and listening material have been added.

Who is it for?

A Way with Words Resource Pack 1 is for adults and upper secondary students at the pre-intermediate and intermediate level. At a slightly higher level, however, students may also welcome the opportunity to revise vocabulary which they already know but rarely use, and in some cases learn a number of important words which have slipped through the net.

A Way with Words is designed to be flexible. It can be used to supplement a coursebook, for a vocabulary option, or to add variety to a listening or reading class.

How is it organised?

The 24 units deal with topics which might typically be included in coursebooks at this level, e.g. travel, crime, relationships, along with a number of linguistically based units which concentrate on important features in vocabulary learning e.g. prefixes and suffixes, and phrasal verbs. The units are not graded in any way, so it is possible to work through the pack in any order, selecting the units or worksheets which will be of most interest and relevance to your students.

What does a unit consist of?

Most units have two, and occasionally three worksheets, with each worksheet containing a series of staged activities around a target group of lexical items. These activities serve to guide the learners to the meaning of the target items in a variety of different ways, and then provide controlled and/or freer practice. Some worksheets may require as little as twenty minutes, others may take twice that long; much will depend on the amount of interest generated by the 'open-ended' activities which allow for freer practice and are a feature of many of the worksheets.

With each worksheet, there is also an accompanying page of teacher's notes containing answer keys, tapescripts, and a list of key words and expressions from the worksheet.

Main Features

- An approach which recognises that vocabulary does not just mean single words: compounds, phrases, and even, on occasion, whole sentences can be items of vocabulary.
- Ideas and activities to help students to become more efficient vocabulary learners. These include suggestions for storing words, remembering them, and recycling them.
- Constant encouragement throughout to make full use of the context, dictionaries, fellow students, the teacher, knowledge of the world, and so on. In this way, students are creatively involved in the learning process and should, over a period of time, become much more self-reliant.
- A wide range of exercise types to keep students motivated and cater for a range of different learning styles.
- An attempt throughout the material to provide students with the opportunity to use the vocabulary they are learning and so facilitate long term retention.
- An accompanying cassette containing recordings for the listening exercises which present new items of vocabulary. It also provides vital help with the pronunciation of many items and adds further variety to the lesson.

Thanks

We would like to extend our thanks once again to all the people who helped us with the original *A Way with Words*, Books 1 and 2: Jeanne McCarten (commissioning editor), Mike McCarthy (advisory editor), Ruth Gairns, Eun Bahng, Michael Swan, and the teachers at The London School of English and The Bell Language Institute, London. Finally, thanks to our desk editors Judith Aguda and Alison Silver, and the rest of the production team at CUP.

For this new Resource Pack, we would also like to thank Lindsay White for setting the project in motion; Brigit Viney for all her work and creativity in adapting and improving the original material to fit this new format; Nóirín Burke and Isabella Wigan for their supervision of the project at its various stages; Liz Driscoll for taking over the sub-editing and Andrew Robinson and the rest of the design and production team at CUP.

Acknowledgements

The authors and publishers are grateful to the authors, publishers and others who have given permission for the use of copyright material identified in the text. It has not been possible to identify the sources of all the material used and in such cases the publishers would welcome information from copyright owners.

Punch for the cartoon on page 15; Addison Wesley Longman Ltd for the extract on page 27 from the *Longman Active Study Dictionary*; AC Press Services for the cartoons on page 37 and page 43 which first appeared in the *Daily Mirror*; Gero Productions Ltd for the advertisement on page 47; London Independent Books for the cartoon on page 51; Solo Syndication Ltd for the article on page 79 which first appeared in the *Daily Mail*; Nigel Luckhurst for the photographs on page 87 (top); Jeremy Pembrey for the photographs on page 87 (bottom).

Illustrations by Simon Turner, Ros Asquith and Amanda Abbitt

Book design by Barnabas Haward

1 a The main purpose of this experiment is to highlight the importance of organisation in vocabulary learning, i.e. if students impose some kind of meaningful order upon the barrage of new words they may encounter, they are more likely to be able to retrieve them from their memory.

Key words

Nouns

accident	life	
apple	line	
ball	nightmare	
bed	peace	
cat	pen	
Christmas	picture	
cloud	pig	
cow	politics	
dog	pyjamas	
door	rabbit	
dream	shape	
examination	sheep	
field	sleep	
flower	sky	
foot	snow	
head	water	
hill	wind	
home	year	
horse		

Adjectives

chock-a-block

1 a Try this experiment. Study the following list of words for one minute and then cover up the list and write down all the words you can remember.

water	life	rabbit	line	home	field	ball	dog	apple
sheep	head	picture	year	sky	chock-a-block	hill		
cloud	horse	shape	pen	wind	pig	cow	foot	door
snow	flower	cat						

b Now read on and answer the *yes/no* questions.

In this experiment did you remember either the first word *water* or the last word *cat*? [*yes/no*] This is very common, because we often remember the information we hear first or the information we hear last.

And what about *chock-a-block*? Did you write that down as well? [*yes/no*] Some people remember this word because it is so unusual.

More important, however, is the *way* that you wrote down your list of words. Did you write down the names of the animals together? [*yes/no*] Most people do, and they sometimes include names of animals that are not on the list. The reason for this is that we automatically group words together in our memory. In other words, the brain is organising the words we learn so that we can remember them more easily. Some people write down *flower* and *field* together because flowers grow in fields; or they write *cloud* and *sky* together because they are both associated with *weather*; or they write down the words in the order they appear on the page (*water, life, rabbit*, etc.). Did you do any of these things? [*yes/no*]

Now compare your answers with a partner's.

(This experiment is adapted from *The Brain Book* by Peter Russell, Routledge & Kegan Paul Ltd.)

2 Try this short experiment. Read each of the following words and write down any other words which immediately come into your mind. The first one has been done for you.

sleep   *bed, dream, peace, nightmare, pyjamas*

accident   ....

examination   ....

politics   ....

Christmas   ....

Compare your answers with a partner's. Are they similar or different? If they are different, why are they different?

1 a With a group of verbs you could also introduce new questions to ask. For example:

– Is it regular or irregular?
– Is it transitive or intransitive?
– Does it have more than one meaning?

Answers

b 2 See tapescript below.
3 'ee-jipt' or /iːdʒɪpt/
4 a noun
5 informal
6 Possible answer: I've been waiting at least half an hour for her.

2 a

explain: give the meaning of a word or idea
concentrate: keep your attention on one thing
choose: select from different possibilities
expand: become or get larger

translate: change from one language into another
improve: get better
revise: study something again
understand: know the meaning of something

b explain → explanation
concentrate → concentration
choose → choice
expand → expansion

translate → translation
improve → improvement
revise → revision
understand → understanding

c 1 translation
2 understand
3 explanation
4 revise

5 expand
6 concentrate
7 chose
8 improve

Tapescript

1 b Listen to the questions about words and phrases and write the answers.

1 What does 'awful' mean?
2 How do you spell 'accident'?
3 There's a country in Africa which is spelt E-G-Y-P-T. How do you pronounce that?
4 Is 'choice' a noun or a verb?
5 Is the word 'guy' formal or informal?
6 How do you use 'at least' in a sentence?

2 b

explain	explanation
concentrate	concentration
choose	choice
expand	expansion
translate	translation
improve	improvement
revise	revision
understand	understanding

Key words and expressions

Nouns	Verbs	Verbs and nouns	Other words and expressions
gap	cover	choose / choice	comfortable
paper clip	fill in (a form)	concentrate / concentration	hang on
recipe	guess	expand / expansion	How do you do?
	look up (a word)	explain / explanation	How do you pronounce (this word)?
	rewrite	improve / improvement	How do you spell (this word)?
	underline	revise / revision	on the tip of my tongue
		translate / translation	What does (this word) mean?
		understand / understanding	

1 a When you learn new words or phrases there is certain information that you need to know. To find it, you can ask questions like these:

What does this word/expression/phrase mean?
What's a '................'?
How do you spell it?
How do you pronounce it?
Is it a noun, a verb (or could it be either?), an adjective, etc.?
How do you use it in a sentence?

b 🔲 Listen to the questions about words and phrases, and write the answers.

Example: 'What does "awful" mean?' '"Awful" means "very bad".'

Now compare your answers with a partner's.

c In pairs, ask each other the questions in **a** to find out about the words and phrases in the box below. If you cannot answer, ask your teacher.

comfortable fill in recipe guess hang on rewrite look something up How do you do? gap cover (something) underline on the tip of my tongue paper clip

d Ask your partner to find a difficult English word in the dictionary. Now ask lots of questions about the word. Can your partner answer all your questions?

2 a The verbs below, on the left, are useful for talking about ways of learning vocabulary. Match the verbs with the correct definitions on the right.

explain	become or get larger
concentrate	change from one language into another
choose	give the meaning of a word or idea
expand	study something again
translate	know the meaning of something
improve	keep your attention on one thing
revise	get better
understand	select from different possibilities

b Write down the nouns that are formed from the verbs in **a**. Use a dictionary to help you. Mark the main stress on both words.

Example: explain → explanation

🔲 Now listen and check your answers.

c Fill in the gaps in the following sentences, using words from **a** and **b**.

1 When I learn a new word, I write down a .... in my own language.
2 If I don't .... a word, I look it up in my dictionary.
3 A picture is often better than an .... of a word.
4 If you don't .... what you learn, you will forget it.
5 Reading is a good way to .... your vocabulary.
6 You can't .... on your work when people are talking around you.
7 I .... this dictionary because it is very small and so I can put it in my pocket.
8 Can I use a dictionary to .... my pronunciation?

d Look again at the sentences in **c**. Do you do 1 and 2 yourself? Do you agree with 3, 4 and 5? And what is the answer to the question in 8? Discuss in groups.

1 a When students record new vocabulary, they tend to write one-word translation equivalents. For many items this will be an accurate and efficient way of recording meaning. For some items, however, translation equivalents will be inaccurate and misleading. For this reason students should be encouraged to consider different ways of recording meaning, and be made aware of the fact that sometimes a translation and/or a definition is needed, plus examples. For example, the word *afraid* has different meanings and different syntactic features governing its use. For this reason example sentences are important:

i) I'm afraid I can't come. (**not** I'm afraid *but* I can't come.)
ii) I'm afraid *of* the dark.

b When students have completed the activity, discuss the answers with the class as a whole. This may take some time, but it will be worthwhile if it helps to establish clear principles about recording meaning. With a monolingual group it can be very interesting to discuss the validity of different translation equivalents.

Answers

1 b A translation would be suitable for: pork, overtake, plug.
Example sentences would be suitable for: too, therefore, on purpose, equals, What's the matter?, leave.
An explanation would be suitable for: pork, launderette, rug.
A picture would be suitable for: overtake, plug, between.

Key words and expressions

Nouns	**Verbs**	**Other words and expressions**
cricket	leave	between
department store	overtake	equals (e.g. x equals y)
dog		I'm afraid
launderette		on purpose
plug		therefore
pork		too (= as well)
rug		under
		What's the matter?

1 a When you learn new words, it is important to write them down to help you remember the meaning. But what is the best way to remember the meaning? Is it best to:

– write a translation?
– write an example sentence in English?
– write an explanation in English or your own language?
– draw a picture?

The answer will be different for different words. Look at these examples:

Translations: department store = 백화점

                     dog = كلب

Example sentences: *I'm afraid* we haven't got the book you want.

Explanations: *Cricket* is a strange English ball-game.

Pictures: under

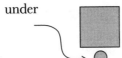

Of course, a translation is not the only way to record the meaning of 'department store' and a picture is not the only way to record the meaning of 'under'. Could you give an explanation of 'department store'? Could you draw a picture of 'cricket'? Talk to your partner about the advantages and disadvantages of these different ways of recording meanings.

b Look at the following words and phrases. What is the best way to record the meaning? In the boxes below write a translation, an example sentence, an explanation or draw a picture for each one. Compare your answers with a partner's.

1	too (= as well)		7	launderette	
2	pork		8	plug	
3	therefore		9	What's the matter?	
4	overtake		10	leave	
5	on purpose		11	between	
6	equals		12	rug	

Answers

1 a Vocabulary networks of this type are a simple and efficient way of recording vocabulary, and you could follow up this activity by asking students to create one of their own.

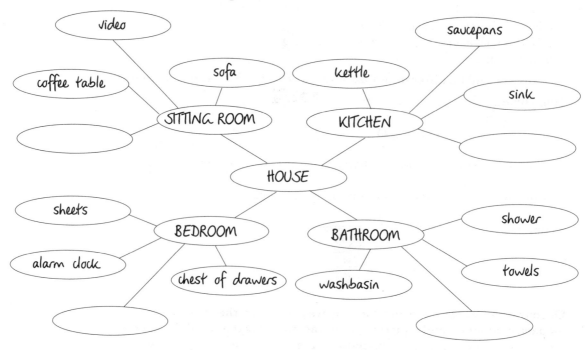

b This is a more abstract and personalised way of making connections between different items of vocabulary. Put students in pairs and encourage them to add more ideas of their own.

2 You may want to start by practising the pronunciation of some difficult items such as *stale* /steɪl/, *cupboard* /kʌbəd/, *wardrobe* /wɔːdrəub/ and *drawer* /drɔː(ə)/.

Possible answers

The shirt was damp, so I put it in the tumble dryer.
The shirt was clean, so I put it in the wardrobe.
The shirt was clean, so I put it in the cupboard.
The plate was broken, so I put it in the bin.
The plate was clean, so I put it in the cupboard.
The plate was dirty, so I put it in the dishwasher.
The ice cream was melting, so I put it in the freezer.
The butter was melting, so I put it in the fridge.
The bread was stale, so I put it in the bin.
The bread was dirty, so I put it in the bin.
The bottle was broken, so I put it in the bin.
The bottle was empty, so I put it in the bin.
The knife was broken, so I put it in the bin.
The knife was clean so, I put it in the drawer.
The knife was dirty so, I put it in the dishwasher.

Key words

Nouns			Verbs	Adjectives
alarm clock	freezer	sink	melt	broken
bin	fridge	sofa		clean
chest of drawers	kettle	towel		damp
coffee table	lounge	tumble dryer		dirty
washbasin	saucepan	video		empty
dishwasher	sheet	wardrobe		stale
cupboard	shower	drawer		

1 a Here is a 'vocabulary network'. Can you complete it with words from the box? Then add one more object for each room.

| saucepans shower sofa towels alarm clock kettle video |
| sheets sink washbasin chest of drawers coffee table |

b In which room do you normally:

listen to music? .... waste time? ....
daydream? .... think about your problems? ....
have arguments? .... feel most relaxed? ....

Now compare your answers with a partner's.

c Why do you have certain things in certain rooms? For example, why not put the television in the bathroom? Why not put the sofa in the kitchen? Think of some more examples and ask your partner to explain them.

2 Make sentences from the words in the box. (There are at least 15 possible sentences.)

Example: The plate was dirty, so I put it in the dishwasher.

	shirt	was	broken,	so I put it in the	drawer.
The	plate		damp,		fridge.
	ice cream		clean,		tumble dryer.
	butter		stale,		cupboard.
	bread		melting,		wardrobe.
	bottle		empty,		freezer.
	knife		dirty,		bin.
					dishwasher.

9

2 Around the house

Answers

1 a
1. a caravan
2. a castle
3. a detached house
4. a tent
5. a cottage
6. terraced houses
7. semi-detached houses
8. a bungalow
9. a block of flats

b
1. a bungalow
2. a flat
3. a caravan
4. a semi-detached house
5. a castle

Tapescript

1 b **Listen to these five people describing their homes and follow the instructions on your worksheet.**

1. We've got three bedrooms, a sitting room and a kitchen and a bathroom. Everything's on the ground floor. In the sitting room we have big French windows so we can walk straight into the garden from there if we want to.
2. As well as the kitchen and bathroom I have one bedroom and a sitting room. I have a lot of neighbours – about fifty. But I only know a few of them – the ones who live above and below me and the ones across the hall.
3. My kitchen, sitting room and bedroom are all in one room. The bed can be changed into a sofa during the day. At the back there is a separate toilet and shower. The number of neighbours I have depends on where I am. Usually it's about ten.
4. Downstairs we have a sitting room, a fairly large dining room and a small kitchen. Upstairs we have two bedrooms and a bathroom. We only have neighbours on one side. They're a very nice young family who moved here a few months ago.
5. I don't really know how many rooms there are here! Some are too dangerous to go in. We just use a few of them – the ones on the south side and the ones next to the tower. In the summer we are open to the general public. We have quite a lot of visitors as it's a very interesting building historically.

Key words and expressions

Nouns	Other words and expressions
bungalow	block of flats
caravan	detached house
castle	semi-detached house
cottage	terraced house
flat	
tent	

Around the house

2

1 a Match the names of types of accommodation in the box with the pictures.

| a block of flats   terraced houses   a castle   a detached house   a tent |
| a cottage   semi-detached houses   a caravan   a bungalow |

① ....

② ....

③ ....

④ ....

⑤ ....

a detached house

⑥ ....

⑦ ....

⑧ ....

⑨

b Listen to these five people describing their homes. Write the type of accommodation each person lives in.

c With a partner, write down one advantage and one disadvantage for each type of accommodation. Then compare your ideas with another pair's.

	Advantage	*Disadvantage*
a block of flats	....	....
terraced houses	....	....
a castle	....	....
a detached house	....	....
a tent	....	....
a cottage	....	....
semi-detached houses	....	....
a caravan	....	....
a bungalow	....	....

d Walk round the class. Find people who have lived or stayed in at least two of these types of accommodation. Which did they prefer and why?

Name	*Two places stayed in*	*Which preferred?*	*Why?*
Anna	tent; caravan	tent	could carry on back

Answers

1 a Make sure students understand what a prefix is before they begin this exercise. It is important to point out that the use of *il- / ir- / im-* is partly predictable but that *un-* (by far the most common of the four prefixes) is not.

The rule is that we use:
il- before the letter 'l'
ir- before the letter 'r'
im- before the letter 'p'
un- before different letters

b **Examples which follow the pattern are:** illogical, irrelevant, imperfect, etc. **One which doesn't is:** unlucky.

Key words

Adjectives
(il)legal
(il)legible
(il)literate
(im)patient
(im)polite
(im)practical
(ir)rational
(ir)regular
(ir)responsible
(un)friendly
(un)satisfactory
(un)tidy

1 a A number of prefixes have the meaning 'not' in English. Look at the following examples using *il- / ir- / im- / un-*. What do they tell you about the use of these prefixes? For example, which kind of words take the prefix *il-*?

  1 It is illegal to drive a car in England without insurance.
  2 You can try and read the letter but my handwriting is almost illegible.
  3 There are still millions of people in the world who are illiterate.
  4 Some people think it is irrational to be frightened of flying.
  5 Journalists often work irregular hours.
  6 I think it is very irresponsible of people to drink and drive.
  7 I'm afraid it's impractical for me to work in two different buildings because I spend more time travelling than working.
  8 In England people think you are being impolite if you don't say please and thank you.

  9 People often get very impatient when they drive in big cities.
10 I'm afraid his work is very unsatisfactory, so we may have to dismiss him.
11 My bedroom is often untidy because I leave my clothes all over the floor.
12 When I started work, I found many of my colleagues were unfriendly.

b Can you think of more examples which either follow the pattern or break it?

2 a Look at the following grid and put a circle (⭕) round the cross (×) which describes your own personality.

Example:

means you are very patient.   **means you are not very patient and not very impatient – i.e. average.**

| patient | ⊗ | × | ⊗ | ⊗ | × | impatient |

means you are quite impatient but not very impatient.

patient	×	×	×	×	×	impatient
polite	×	×	×	×	×	impolite
practical	×	×	×	×	×	impractical
rational	×	×	×	×	×	irrational
responsible	×	×	×	×	×	irresponsible
tidy	×	×	×	×	×	untidy
friendly	×	×	×	×	×	unfriendly

b Now compare your grid with your partner's. Have you got similar personalities?

3 Prefixes

Answers

1 a The prefix 're-' cannot be attached to every verb but it is a very generative prefix, and students are pleasantly surprised to discover that they can often guess the correct answers in **a** and generate further examples of their own in **b**.

Possible answers

1 Are they going to rebuild it?
2 Are you going to redo it?
3 Are they reopening somewhere else?
4 Yes, it needs reorganising.
5 Couldn't you rearrange your appointment?

b Some other examples with 're-' are:

reconsider, reconstruct, refill, refresh, regain, rehouse, rename, replay, reprint, rethink

2 a
over-	overcrowded, overcharge, overworked, overripe
de-	defrosting, decaffeinated, deodorant, dehumanised
mis-	mismanagement
anti-	anti-social, antifreeze, antiseptically
under-	understaffed, underequipped

The meanings are:

over-	means *too much* of something
de-	often means that something is removed
mis-	often means *badly* or *incorrectly*
anti-	usually means *against*
under-	is the opposite of *over-*. It means *not enough*.

Tapescript

2 a Listen to the conversation and follow the instructions on your worksheet.

A: I don't know why it is but whenever I go to that supermarket in Sokely I come back feeling so anti-social!

B: I've noticed.

A: Well, it's just so overcrowded on a Saturday afternoon. You queue for half an hour and then they get it wrong and try to overcharge you. It's enough to drive you mad.

B: Don't they have machines to do the calculating for them?

A: Of course they do, but they're really ancient and don't seem to work properly. You can't really blame the staff; they're overworked and tired. The whole place is understaffed and underequipped.

B: Anyway, did you get everything?

A: No, no, I didn't. All the potatoes were packed in five-kilo bags. I mean – who wants five kilos of potatoes? And the freezers were defrosting all over the floor so I decided against frozen food. And also, they didn't have any decaffeinated coffee, and all the peaches were overripe so I got apples instead.

B: That's OK: it doesn't matter.

A: And, I'm afraid they only had that deodorant that smells like antifreeze, so I didn't bother getting any. It really is an awful place! I hate it! Talk about mismanagement!

B: Well why don't you go to that hypermarket in Conborough instead? It's enormous and ultramodern, with masses of parking space.

A: Yes ... but it's so antiseptically clean and sort of dehumanised. There's no atmosphere, no character. It's worse than this one ...

Key words

Verbs		Adjectives		Nouns	Adverbs
defrost	reorganise	anti-social	underequipped	antifreeze	antiseptically
overcharge	reread	decaffeinated	understaffed	deodorant	
rearrange	rewrite	dehumanised		mismanagement	
rebuild		overcrowded			
redo		overripe			
reopen		overworked			

1 a The prefix *re-* can be used with certain verbs, where it often has the meaning 'to do something again'.

Example: I'm going to reread that chapter. = I'm going to read it again.

Write a logical response to the following sentences, including a suitable verb with the prefix *re-*.

Example: A: I'm sorry but I can't read your essay.

B: Do you want me to rewrite it?

1 A: They knocked down that house last month.

B: ....

2 A: My teacher said my homework was terrible.

B: ....

3 A: That shop's closing down next month.

B: ....

4 A: The department is in a terrible mess – it's so inefficient.

B: ....

5 A: If I meet you on Tuesday, I won't be able to keep my appointment at the dentist's.

B: ....

b Can you think of more verbs where you can use the prefix *re-*?

2 a 🔲 Listen to the conversation between two people talking about their local supermarket and write down all the words you hear which begin with the five prefixes below.

over-	....	....	....	....
de-	....	....	....	....
mis-	....	....	....	....
anti-	....	....	....	....
under-	....	....	....	....

b Discuss the meanings of these prefixes with your partner.

c Now think of other words which begin with these prefixes. Make sure the prefixes in your words have the same meaning as the examples from the cassette. (Use a dictionary if necessary.)

d With a partner, write a short dialogue in which you include an example of each of the five prefixes above. Then read it to another pair and listen to their dialogue. Note down any new words they use.

COMPUTER CENTRE

'This one frankly admits it's overpriced.'

Answers

1 a

Nouns	Adjectives
climate	climatic
sun	sunny
ice	icy
fog	foggy
mist	misty
shower	showery
warmth	warm
humidity	humid
heat	hot

b You could put these phrases on individual slips of paper, give each student one slip of paper, and tell them to move round the class until they find a suitable phrase to complete their sentence. At the end highlight this use of *get* (= become) and add further examples, e.g. *getting warm/cold/light*. Also check the pronunciation of *mild* /maɪld/ and *pour* /pɔː/.

One possible set of answers is:

It was getting hot, so I decided to sit in the shade.
It was very bright, so I put on my sunglasses.
It was getting dark, so I put the lights on.
It was beginning to rain, so I put my umbrella up.

It was incredibly humid, so I decided to have a swim.
It was pouring with rain, so I couldn't go out.
It was quite mild, so I didn't take my overcoat.
It was extremely icy, so I decided not to go by car.

c Encourage students to use the new vocabulary in different permutations. For example:

It was beginning to get dark.
It was incredibly bright.
It was quite hot.

2 a There may be lots of places like this, but we had Korea in mind.

Key words and expressions

Nouns	Adjectives	Verbs	Other words and expressions
climate	bright	pour (with rain)	extremely
fog	clear	put (the lights) on	incredibly
heat	climatic	put up (an umbrella)	in the shade
humidity	cold	snow	
ice	dark		
mist	dry		
overcoat	foggy		
shade	fresh		
shower	hot		
sun	humid		
sunglasses	icy		
thunderstorm	marvellous		
warmth	mild		
	misty		
	pleasant		
	rain		
	showery		
	sunny		
	warm		

1 a Complete the table with the correct adjectives and nouns. Check the meanings of any unfamiliar words in the dictionary.

Nouns	Adjectives
climate	....
sun	....
ice	....
fog	....
mist	....
shower	....
warmth	....
....	humid
....	hot

b Different places have different climates. Make sentences from the words in the table.

It was	getting hot, very bright, getting dark, beginning to rain, incredibly humid, pouring with rain, quite mild, extremely icy,	so I	put my umbrella up. put the lights on. decided to sit in the shade. didn't take my overcoat. couldn't go out. put on my sunglasses. decided to have a swim. decided not to go by car.

c Think of more things you did because of the weather (like the right-hand column of the table in **b**) and get your partner to finish your sentences like this:

You: I bought a long cool drink because …
Your partner: … because it was incredibly hot and humid.

2 a Read the following description of the typical weather in January, April and August in a particular country. Try to guess where it might be.

In January it often gets extremely cold, occasionally as low as –20°C. However, it's always wonderfully clear, bright and sunny at this time of year, and the air seems to be dry even if it snows.

There's a very definite spring season in April. It's quite warm and sunny but it may be showery and it gets misty sometimes. Of course, this is when all the plants start flowering. It's marvellous.

August is not very pleasant at all because it's incredibly hot (about 30°C) and humid. Sometimes there's a thunderstorm and it pours with rain for a while. This makes the air a bit fresher – but not for long.

b Write about the typical weather in your country (or another country) in January, April and August.

Answers

1 a Students usually enjoy working on these puzzles individually.

S	T	O	R	E	T	G	R	A	P	E
P	E	P	P	E	R	A	N	N	I	S
E	L	M	O	T	I	R	U	E	N	T
C	A	U	L	I	F	L	O	W	E	R
A	N	S	T	R	C	I	T	H	A	A
R	O	H	B	E	O	C	H	S	P	W
R	A	R	E	N	O	P	A	N	P	B
O	G	O	I	W	E	E	S	O	L	E
T	R	O	D	A	P	A	D	I	E	R
I	N	M	R	E	S	C	U	F	O	R
M	E	L	O	N	C	H	E	R	R	Y

Tapescript

b Listen and repeat the words.

grape   pineapple   strawberry   pear   cherry   melon
cauliflower   mushroom   carrot   onion   peas   pepper   garlic

Key words

Nouns
carrot
cauliflower
cherry
garlic
grape
melon
mushroom
onion
peach
pear
peas
pepper
pineapple
strawberry

1 a The names of all the fruit and vegetables below can be found in the puzzle.
The words may be horizontal, vertical, or diagonal. How many can you find?

```
S T O R E T G R A P E
P E P P E R A N N I S
E L M O T I R U E N T
C A U L I F L O W E R
A N S T R C I T H A A
R O H B E O C H S P W
R A R E N O P A N P B
O G O I W E E S O L E
T R O D A P A D I E R
I N M R E S C U F O R
M E L O N C H E R R Y
```

b ⌨ Listen and repeat the names of the fruit and vegetables that appear in
the puzzle. Did you find them all?

c Now try to think of eight more kinds of fruit, eight more kinds of vegetable,
eight kinds of meat, and complete the chart.

Fruit	Vegetables	Meat

d Do you find all these fruits, vegetables and kinds of meat in your country?
Which are the least common? Make a list and then compare your lists in
groups.

Answers

1 a **Students should be able to deduce the meaning of unknown items, so do not preteach them. The order is usually:**

1	decide to go out for a meal	8	have the main course
2	book a table	9	have dessert
3	go to the restaurant	10	ask for the bill
4	sit down	11	pay the bill
5	look at the menu	12	give the waiter a tip
6	order the meal	13	leave the restaurant
7	have the starter		

b **The differences are:**

They didn't book a table.
They asked to move to another table.
They ordered aperitifs.
They ordered wine.
They had some coffee and brandy.
They didn't give the waiter a tip.

2 a
1 coffee
2 steak or beef
3 pepper
4 onions
5 garlic
6 vinegar or lemon juice
7 butter or ice or chocolate
8 alcohol

Tapescript

1 b **Listen to the conversation and follow the instructions on your worksheet.**

W: … and then of course we went out last night.
M: Oh yes, what was it like?
W: Very nice … I'd definitely recommend it. But if you want to go, you'll probably need to book, because it gets very busy, especially at the weekend. We didn't bother as it was a Tuesday, but even so, there were quite a few people there.
M: And the food was good?
W: Yeah, excellent. We had a slight problem to start with because they put us at a table near a window which was a bit draughty, but when we asked for another table they were very nice about it, and after that the service was great. Anyway, we had an aubergine dish to start, with a yoghurt sauce and masses of garlic. And then for the main course, I had lamb, which was very tender, and the others had some kind of casserole – pieces of pork marinated in oil and herbs and lemon juice (mmm!) and then cooked with onions and peppers and so on. And we finished with one of those sticky sweet desserts made from nuts and honey.
M: Mmm. Sounds nice. Is it pricey?
W: Well, it's about twenty-five pounds each I guess, which isn't bad when you consider that we had a bottle of wine, coffee and Greek brandy at the end of the meal, and the other two had aperitifs as well and service is included so you don't need to give a tip.
M: Yeah, that's not bad these days. I think I'll give it a try. Where did you say it was exactly?

Key words

Nouns		**Verbs**		**Adjectives**
bill	restaurant	book (a table)	order (a meal)	medium rare
dessert	starter	chop	pour	rare
hangover	tip	cry	smell	
main course	waiter	leave (= allow to remain)	sneeze	
meal		melt		
menu		mix		

Food and restaurants 5

1 a When you go out for a meal, you usually do a number of things. Look at the list of actions below and put them into the correct order. The first one has been done for you.

look at the menu ....
give the waiter a tip ....
have dessert ....
pay the bill ....
book a table ....
decide to go out for a meal ....1.....
leave the restaurant ....
have the starter ....
go to the restaurant ....
have the main course ....
sit down ....
order the meal ....
ask for the bill ....

And would Sir like some garlic bread?

b [cassette icon] Listen to the story of an evening in a restaurant. In what ways is the order of events different from the order in **a**?

c Of course you do not always follow the sequence in **a**. What happens in:

a hamburger (fast food) restaurant?
a pub?
a restaurant or bar in your country?

2 a What are the people talking about in the following sentences? In some cases there may be more than one answer.

1 I never have it late at night because it keeps me awake.
2 I like it rare or medium rare.
3 It makes you sneeze if it goes up your nose.
4 They often make you cry when you chop them.
5 I often use it in cooking but it makes your breath smell.
6 Just mix it with oil and salt, and pour it over the salad.
7 If you leave it in the sun, it will melt.
8 It makes me happy, and then gives me a hangover.

b Look at the use of the following constructions:

| make | + | noun or pronoun | + | adjective or infinitive | *sentence 8*
 sentences 3, 4 and 5 |

| keep | + | noun or pronoun | + | adjective | *sentence 1* |

| give | + | noun or pronoun | + | noun | *sentence 8* |

Using these constructions, make some more sentences.

Examples: 'Smoking makes me cough.' 'Wine gives me a headache.'

Answers

1 a Some possibilities are:

landing/boarding/birthday/membership/identity	*card*
news/examination/toilet/file/note/writing	*paper*
waiting/living/sick/stock/dressing/cloak/bath/bed	*room*
wheel/easy/electric/rocking/deck/push	*chair*

2 a The objects in the pictures are:

1 a knife sharpener
2 a food processor
3 a potato peeler
4 a coffee pot/percolator
5 a tin opener
6 a dishwasher
7 a cheese grater

b
1 a washing machine
2 a hammer
3 a corkscrew
4 a saw/an axe
5 an iron
6 a screwdriver
7 scissors
8 a drill/a hole punch
9 a camera
10 a key

Key words

Nouns	Verbs	Adjectives
alarm clock	babysit	easy-going
axe		
bottle opener		
camera		
cheese grater		
coffee percolator		
coffee pot		
corkscrew		
credit card		
dishwasher		
drill		
food processor		
hammer		
hole punch		
iron		
key		
knife		
knife sharpener		
potato peeler		
saw		
scissors		
screwdriver		
tin opener		
washing machine		

Compounds 6

1 Look at these examples of compounds:

One word	+	One word	=	New word
alarm	+	clock	=	alarm clock (a compound noun)
easy	+	going	=	easy-going (a compound adjective)
baby	+	sit	=	babysit (a compound verb)

The most common type of compound is a compound noun. You can often create compound nouns in English by using your first language and a little imagination. For example, how many compound nouns can you find using the following words? (Use a dictionary to check your answers.)

Example: ...*credit*... card .... paper .... room .... chair

2 a In English you can build some compound nouns from two nouns like this:

A *bottle opener* is a thing you use to open bottles.

Can you complete these compound nouns and match them with the correct pictures?

a tin
a knife
a coffee
a potato
a dish
a food
a cheese

① ....

⑤ ....

④ ....

⑥ ....

⑦ ....

Check in your dictionary to see which of your words exist in English.

b Of course, there are lots of gadgets and tools around the house for which we have a word which does not follow this pattern.

Example: a *food cutter* is called a *knife* in English, **not** a *food cutter*.

What are the real words in English for the following invented words?

1 a clothes washer ....
2 a nail hitter ....
3 a cork remover ....
4 a wood cutter ....
5 a clothes flattener ....
6 a screw turner ....
7 a paper cutter ....
8 a hole maker ....
9 a picture taker ....
10 a door locker ....

© Cambridge University Press 1996

Answers

1 a
hang gliding
water skiing
weight training
oil painting
sightseeing
parachute jumping
rock climbing
stamp collecting
rifle shooting
window shopping
dressmaking
bird-watching
windsurfing
sunbathing
motorcycling
flower arranging

2 a Probable answers are:

lunch (time) table
shop (assistant) manager
toilet (paper) towel
phone (number) plate
wheel (chair) person
burglar (alarm) clock
window (shopping) list
bed (room) service
table (tennis) racket
soft (ware) house
identity (card) board

Key words

Nouns
Hobbies and leisure activities
bird-watching
dressmaking
flower arranging
hang gliding
motorcycling
oil painting
parachute jumping
rifle shooting
rock climbing
sightseeing
stamp collecting
sunbathing
water skiing
weight training
windsurfing
window shopping

Others
alarm clock
assistant manager
bedroom
burglar alarm
cardboard
chairperson
identity card
lunch-time
number-plate
paper towel
phone number
room service
shop assistant
shopping list
software
speed limit
table tennis
tennis racket
timetable
toilet paper
top speed
warehouse
wheelchair

1 a Match words in the left-hand box with words in the right-hand box to form 16 compound nouns describing different hobbies and leisure activities.

hang	rifle
water	window
weight	dress
oil	bird
sight	wind
parachute	sun
rock	motor
stamp	flower

watching shooting gliding painting
cycling seeing making climbing
jumping collecting surfing arranging
skiing shopping training bathing

b Move round the class and find out if anyone does any of these things. If so, find out more about this particular hobby or activity.

2 a Can you find a word to go in each of the brackets below, so that you have a compound with the word before the brackets and a compound with the word after the brackets?

Example: top (...*speed*...) limit

1	lunch	(..................)	table	7	window	(..................)	list
2	shop	(..................)	manager	8	bed	(..................)	service
3	toilet	(..................)	towel	9	table	(..................)	racket
4	phone	(..................)	plate	10	soft	(..................)	house
5	wheel	(..................)	person	11	identity	(..................)	board
6	burglar	(..................)	clock				

b Now write sentences which combine both of the compounds in each case.

Example: You can't go at *top speed* in most cars in Britain because the *speed limit* is only 70 m.p.h.

Answers

1 a
1. How long are you staying? (delete *time*)
2. I saw him *last* night. (or *yesterday evening*)
3. I didn't sleep very well *last* night.
4. I haven't seen her *for* three weeks.
5. What are you doing *tonight*? (or *this evening*)
6. When did you arrive *in* London?
7. I arrived two days *ago*.
8. What time shall we meet? (delete *us*)
9. I'm going there next month. (delete *the*)
10. Before *leaving* we must get some souvenirs.
11. I haven't seen her in the last *few* days. (or *recently* or *lately*)
12. I'm going to the shop but I'll be back *in* half an hour.

2 a
1. from time to time
2. on time
3. had a great time / had the time of our lives
4. for the time being / for a time
5. in good time

b **All of these replies from B would require some kind of acknowledgement from A, either to register pleasure or simply understanding. In these examples 'I see' or 'Oh, good' would seem to be the most likely and appropriate.**

Here are some possible answers:

1. I thought so.
2. Maybe he's got lost.
3. Oh, good.
4. I see.
5. Oh, good.

Tapescript

1 b **Listen and check your answers.**

1. How long are you staying?
2. I saw him last night. *or* I saw him yesterday evening.
3. I didn't sleep very well last night.
4. I haven't seen her for three weeks.
5. What are you doing tonight?
6. When did you arrive in London?
7. I arrived two days ago.
8. What time shall we meet?
9. I'm going there next month.
10. Before leaving we must get some souvenirs.
11. I haven't seen her in the last few days. *or* I haven't seen her recently.
12. I'm going to the shop but I'll be back in half an hour.

Key words and expressions

Adverbs	Prepositions	Adjectives	Time expressions		Other expressions
ago	before (leaving)	punctual	for a time	next week/month	have a good time
normally	for (three weeks)		for the time being	on time	have the time of our lives
occasionally	in (half an hour)		from time to time	tonight	How long are you staying?
recently	since (last week,		in good time	yesterday evening	What time shall we meet?
usually	1985, Monday)		in the last few days		
			last night/week		

Time 7

1 a There are mistakes in all the sentences below. Try to find the mistake in each of the twelve sentences and then compare your sentences with your partner's.

1 How long time are you staying?
2 I saw him yesterday night.
3 I didn't sleep very well this night.
4 I haven't seen her since three weeks.
5 What are you doing this night?
6 When did you arrive to London?
7 I arrived two days before.
8 What time shall we meet us?
9 I'm going there the next month.
10 Before to leave we must get some souvenirs.
11 I haven't seen her in the last days.
12 I'm going to the shop but I'll be back after half an hour.

She's a bit ahead of her time.

b Now listen carefully to the correct sentences and check your answers.

2 a We often confirm statements and questions by repeating what someone has said, but we use a different word or phrase. For example:

A: You've been here for ten years?
B: Yes, since 1987.

A: It's a beautiful place, isn't it?
B: Yes, lovely.

Now you respond to the following statements or questions by rephrasing the sentence. You will find the expressions you need in these definitions from a dictionary entry for *time*.

1 A: It happens occasionally.
   B: Yes, ...
2 A: He's normally punctual, isn't he?
   B: Yes, he's usually ....
3 A: You enjoyed the holiday, then?
   B: Yes, we ....
4 A: Are you going to stay in the flat for a while?
   B: Yes, ...
5 A: We should get there before it starts.
   B: Oh yes, we'll be there ....

|He comes here **from time to time**. (=occasionally)|*Do the trains ever run* **on time** (=at the right time) *here?*|*The people came in* **two at a time**. (=in groups of two)|*I've told you* **time after time/time and again** (=repeatedly) *not to do that.* **7** [C *often plural*] a period: *in ancient times*|*in Queen Victoria's time*|*We had a good time* (= enjoyed ourselves) *at the party.*|*a writer who is* **ahead of her time** (=has ideas too modern or original for the period in which she lives) | **At one time** (=formerly) *I used to like her, but not anymore.* | *He lived* **for a time** (= for a short period) *in Spain.* **8** [U] the rate of speed of a piece of music: *You* **beat time** *and I'll play.*|*The players at the back aren't* **keeping time. 9 at the same time** in spite of this: yet: *He can be very rude, but at the same time I can't help liking him.* **10 for the time being** for a limited period: *I'll let you keep the book for the time being, but I'll want it back next week.* **11 have no time for** *infml* to dislike **12 have the time of one's life** to have a very enjoyable experience **13 in good time: a** at the right time **b** early enough **14 in one's own good time** *infml* when one is ready and not before **15 in time** early enough: *we must make sure we arrive in time to get a good seat.*

(From the Longman Active Study Dictionary)

b Can you add another word or two from A to finish each conversation?

Answers

1 a **Most British people would answer something like this:**

a baby = 0 to 2 (approximately)
a child/chilhood = 2 to 12 (approximately)
an adolescent/adolescence = 14 to 17 (approximately)
a teenager = 13 to 19
(a) youth = 13 to 18 (approximately)
an adult = 16/18 upwards
a pensioner = after 60 or 65 usually
youth = teens to early twenties
middle age(d) = between 35 and 60 (depending on *your* age)
old (age) = after 70 (approximately – depending on *your* age)
elderly = after 70 (approximately – depending on *your* age)

2 a **The permutations are endless here, so it may be advisable to restrict the number of expressions to about twelve per student. Examples include:**

on Tuesday morning
just after seven o'clock
last night
yesterday evening
almost two years ago
just over four weeks
in 1975
last Christmas
in the afternoon
on April 10
at night

Key words and expressions

Nouns	Verbs	Adjectives	Expressions with time	Other expressions
adolescence	begin	elderly	about 3 weeks ago	get drunk
adolescent	cry	middle-aged	almost (2 years ago)	get into trouble
adult	end	old	at (4 o'clock)	go bald
baby	crawl	young	in (January, 1993)	lose weight
child	last		just after (10 o'clock)	make (a lot of) money
childhood	retire		just over (2 years)	make a will
middle age	worry (about something)		on (Tuesday)	put on weight
old age				take exams
pensioner				
teenager				
youth				

1 a Using the scale below, indicate the time period for each of the words in the boxes below:

countable nouns:
> a baby   a child   an adolescent   a teenager   a youth
> an adult   a pensioner

uncountable nouns:
> childhood   adolescence   youth   middle age   old age

adjectives:
> young   middle-aged   elderly   old

Example: teenager

```
.__.__.__.__.__.__.__.__.__.__.__.__.__.__.__.__.
0   5   10  15  20  25  30  35  40  45  50  55  60  65  70  75  80
```

Compare your answers with a partner's. These constructions may help you:

'Adolescence begins at 14 (years old) and ends at 17.'
'Adolescence lasts from 14 to 17.'
'I think you are an adolescent from 14 to 17.'

b Which of these periods do you associate with the following? (Look up new words in a dictionary and then discuss your answers in groups.)

Example: 'putting on weight'   'Many people put on weight between 35 and 50.'

1 going bald
2 getting drunk
3 crying a lot
4 putting on weight
5 trying to lose weight
6 getting into trouble
7 retiring
8 worrying about money
9 making a lot of money
10 crawling on the floor
11 taking exams
12 making a will

2 a How many *past* time expressions can you make from the following table?

Example: 'about seven months ago' from columns *2, 3, 4, 5*

1	2	3	4	5	6	7
at on in	about just after just over almost	4 7 10 12 2	days hours minutes months weeks years o'clock	ago April 10 last 1975 Tuesday yesterday	the	afternoon Christmas evening January month morning night week year

b Give your partner a list of column numbers from the table and see if he or she can make a correct time expression in English. For example:

You: One, seven.
Your partner: At Christmas (*or* In January).

Answers

1 a
1 bus stop
2 T-junction
3 traffic lights
4 main road
5 pedestrian crossing
6 roundabout

b The map should look like this when you have finished:

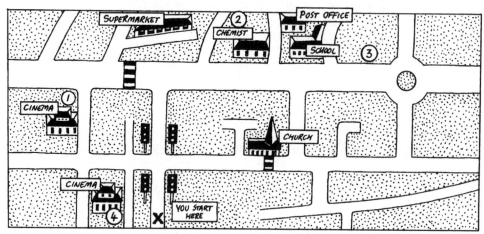

c and **d** See Tapescript **1 b** below. The missing words are in italics.

e These are possible sets of directions:

1 Now you are outside the restaurant. Go back down this road, turn right and then turn left at the traffic lights. When you come to the main road, turn left and then turn right just after the pedestrian crossing. Take the first road on your right and you will see the supermarket on your left.
2 Now you are outside the supermarket. Go back down this road and turn left. When you come to the main road, turn left and then take the second road on your left. The post office is on the right, almost opposite the chemist.

Tapescript

1 b Look at the map and find the place which says 'You start here'. Now follow the directions.

1 Go along this road, turn left at the *traffic lights*, um, and then *take* the, oh, the second on the right. You'll see the *bus stop* on the *left-hand* side, just *after* the cinema.

Mark the bus stop on your map and follow the next set of directions. Remember you are now at the bus stop.

2 Now you keep going along this road in the same direction. Then you turn right at the *main road* and then take the *second* on the left. You'll see the *bank* about halfway along on the right side of the road.

Mark the bank on your map and follow the next set of directions.

3 Go *back* down this road, er, turn left and then keep going for, er, oh, about five minutes. The *underground's* on your left er … er, it's just *before* you get to the *roundabout*.

Mark the underground on your map and follow the final set of directions.

4 OK. Take the road *on your right* at the roundabout, and then turn right again when you *get* to a *T-junction*. Now when you've done that, you've got to *follow* the road, *past* a church, over a *set* of traffic lights, and then take the *next* road on your left. The *restaurant's* about *halfway* along on the *right-hand* side.

Mark the restaurant on your map.

Key words and expressions

Nouns		Verbs	Giving directions	
bus stop	roundabout	get = (reach)	halfway along	take the first/second (turning)
main road	T-junction	go (along/back/past)	just after/before	turn left/right (at/into)
pedestrian crossing	traffic lights		keep going	
			on the left-/right- (hand side)	
			opposite	

1 a Use the words in the box to form six new words or phrases below.

| road   about   junction   stop   lights   crossing |

1 bus ....
2 T-..................
3 traffic ....

4 main ....
5 pedestrian ....
6 round..................

b 🔲 Look at the map below and then listen to the four passages on the cassette. As you listen, follow the directions on the map and follow the instructions at the end of each passage.

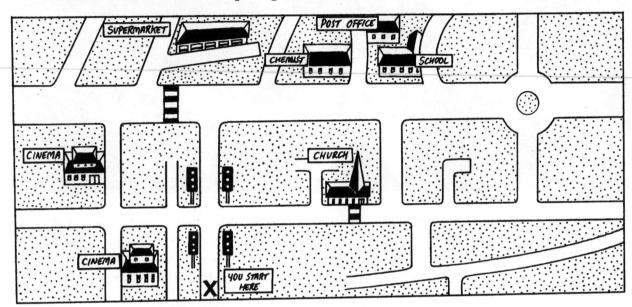

C Read the directions below and try to fill in the missing words.

1 Go along this road, turn left at the ...., and then .... the second on the right. You'll see the .... on the ....-.................. side, just .... the cinema.

2 Now you keep going along this road in the same direction. Then you turn right at the .... and then take the .... on the left. You'll see the .... about halfway along on the .... side of the road.

3 Go .... down this road, turn left and then keep going for about five minutes. The ....'s on your left, it's just .... you get to the ....

4 OK. Take the road .... your right at the roundabout, and then turn right again when you .... to a ....-................... Now when you've done that, you've got to .... the road, ... a church, over a .... of traffic lights, and then take the .... road on your left. The ....'s about .... along on the ....-.................. side.

d Listen to the directions again and check your answers to **C**.

e Now work with your partner and *you* give the directions. How do you get to:
1 the supermarket?
2 the Post Office?

(Remember, you are at the restaurant now.)

Answers

1 a

1	an ambulance	4	a lorry	7	a bike
2	a coach	5	a motorbike
3	a bus	6	a van

b The order of the sentences is: 6, 2, 4, 1, 5, 3.

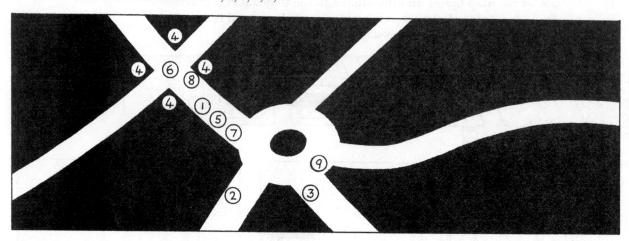

Whose fault was the accident? Possible answers are: the lorry driver; the car driver; the van driver.

Key words and expressions

Nouns	**Verbs**	**Other words and expressions**
ambulance	brake	at the bottom/top
bike	change (to red)	badly (injured)
bus	come (out of)	opposite direction
coach	crash (into something)	parked cars
lorry	damage	slightly (damaged)
motorbike	hit	stationary
pedestrian crossing	injure	the wrong way
roundabout	knock (someone) down	
traffic lights	roll	
van	stop	
	swerve	
	wait	

1 a Match the words and pictures below.

> a van   a lorry   a bus   a bike   a coach   a motorbike   an ambulance

b Here is a description of an accident, but the order of the events is mixed up. Number 6 is the first event, but can you put the others in order? Use the map in **C** to help you.

1   On the way it hit several parked cars which were slightly damaged and then it knocked down a man on the pedestrian crossing. He was quite badly injured.

2   A red car, which was coming from the opposite direction, was trying to get to the traffic lights before they changed to red. When the driver saw the lorry, he braked but he could not stop in time.

3   The van finally stopped when it crashed into a stationary coach which was waiting to come out of Radcliffe Avenue.

4   The lorry swerved and hit a van which was parked in Windsor Hill, very close to the traffic lights. The van began to roll down the hill towards the roundabout.

5   At the bottom of the hill, it started going round the roundabout the wrong way and hit a motorbike coming out of Cambourne Road in front of it.

6   There is a 'no right turn' sign at the top of Windsor Hill. However, a lorry came up Windsor Hill and turned right at the traffic lights.

C Now mark the following on the map:

1   Windsor Hill
2   Cambourne Road
3   Radcliffe Avenue
4   the traffic lights
5   the pedestrian crossing
6   the top of the hill
7   the bottom of the hill
8   where the van started
9   where the van stopped

Whose fault was the accident?

d Now draw a diagram of the accident on the map. Can your partner use your diagram to explain what happened?

Answers

1 a

Infinitive	Past tense	Past participle
to get	got	got
to ride	rode	ridden
to drive	drove	driven
to take	took	taken
to catch	caught	caught

b The *wrong* answers are:

1 a car
2 a car
3 a motorbike
4 a bike
5 a taxi

c The most natural answers are:

1 take a taxi
2 (any correct sentence with *ride* or *drive*)
3 got on / off
4 took a plane / caught a plane
5 got into the car

2 a

1 I want a ticket to go to Manchester but not to come back again. (coach station or railway station)
2 (at a coach station)
3 Does this train go all the way to my destination? (railway station)
4 Can I buy food and drink on the train? (railway station)
5 Do I have to pay if my luggage weighs more than an agreed weight? (at an airport)
6 Where is the place in the station to buy tickets? (coach station or railway station)
7 How much is a ticket to go to Glasgow and come back again? (coach station or railway station)
8 (probably on the underground)
9 Exactly where in the station do I get on the train? (railway station)
10 Can I get a train to Edinburgh with a special place to sleep during the journey? (railway station)
11 I am looking for the office where they keep things that people have lost in the station or on the train/coach. (railway station or coach station)
12 Do I need to pay for a special ticket with a seat number or will there be enough places on the train or coach for everyone to sit down? (railway station or coach station)

Key words

Nouns	Verbs
buffet car	catch (a bus)
coach	change (trains)
excess baggage	drive (a car)
line	get into (a car)
lost property	get off (a bus)
platform	get on (a bus)
return	get out of (a car)
single	miss (a bus)
sleeper	reserve (a seat)
ticket office	ride (a horse)
	take (a taxi)

1 a Look at the verbs in this table and fill in the *past tense* and *past participle* for each one. Use your dictionary to check if you are not sure.

Infinitive	Past tense	Past participle
to get		
to ride		
to drive		
to take		
to catch		

b The verbs in **a** are often used with particular forms of transport. In each of the following there is a form of transport which does not go with the verb. Which one?

Example:

to get	into out of	a car a rowing boat a bicycle a taxi

In this example, *bicycle* is wrong, but you can use the other nouns. Now look at the verbs and nouns below and indicate the wrong word.

1
to get	on off	a bicycle a horse a train a car

2
to ride		a horse a motorbike a car a bike

3
to drive		a train a car a taxi a motorbike

4
to take		a bike a train a plane a taxi

5
to	catch miss	a train a bus a taxi

c Complete these sentences using the verbs and nouns from **a** and **b**.

1 I missed the bus this morning so I had to ....
2 I'd like to learn how to...
3 The train arrived at the station and we ....
4 I had to get from London to Madrid very quickly so I ....
5 I hit my head on the roof when I ....

2 a What do the following sentences mean? Where would you expect to hear them?

1 Can I have a *single* to Manchester?
2 What time does the *coach* leave?
3 Do I have to *change*?
4 Is there a *buffet car*?
5 Do I have to pay *excess baggage*?
6 Where's the *ticket office*?
7 How much is a *return* to Glasgow?
8 Which *line* do I take?
9 Which *platform*?
10 Can I get a *sleeper* to Edinburgh?
11 Where's the *lost property* office?
12 Do I need to *reserve a seat*?

STATION

Is there a sleeper on this train?

No, just a driver.

b Work in pairs. Take it in turns to ask the questions in **a** and provide logical answers. For example:

A: Is there a *buffet car*?
B: No. Not on this train.

c Now do the exercise again. This time use the words in italics in **a** to ask different questions. For example:

A: Where's the *buffet car*?
B: It's that way.

Answers

1 a
1 ... hang it up.
2 ... I'll wake him up.
3 OK, I'll turn it up.
4 Yes, I'll turn it off.
5 Yes, I'll put it out.
6 OK, I'll tidy it up.
7 OK, I'll turn it on.
8 Yes, I'll take it out.

b **Some possible answers are:**
1 That music is very loud.
2 The light's off.
3 Your coat's dirty.
4 These tomatoes are bad.

d *washing machine:* turn it on/off, switch it on/off
stereo: turn it on/off, turn it up/down, switch it on/off
TV: turn it on/off, turn it up/down, switch it on/off
kettle: turn it on/off, switch it on/off
rubbish: throw it away, take it out, put it out
money: take it out
clothes: tidy them up, hang them up, take them off, throw them away
computer: turn it on/off, switch it on/off
things: tidy them up, throw them away, take them out, put them out
fire: turn it on/off, turn it up/down, switch it on/off, put it out

Key words and expressions

Nouns	Verbs
computer	hang (something) up
fire	put (something) out
kettle	switch (something) off
money	switch (something) on
rubbish	take (something) off
stereo	take (something) out (of)
things	throw (something) away
TV	tidy (something) up
washing machine	turn (something) down
	turn (something) off
	turn (something) on
	turn (something) up
	wake (someone) up

Phrases and phrasal verbs 10

1 a Look at the verbs in the box and read A's remarks and questions. Complete
B's answers, using the verbs in the box.

tidy something up	turn something on	turn something off
hang something up	take something out	switch something off
turn something up	put something out	wake someone up

Example: A: This light is very bright   B OK, ...I'll switch it off.........................

1   A: Your coat's on the floor.   B: OK, I'll ....
2   A: Is John still asleep?   B: Yes, ...
3   A: I can't hear the radio.   B: ....
4   A: Is that tap still running?   B: ....
5   A: Is that cigarette still burning?   B: ....
6   A: This room is in a mess.   B: ....
7   A: There's a good programme on TV.   B: ....
8   A: Is the ice cream still in the freezer?   B: ....

b Now write A's words in these dialogues:

1   A: ....   B: OK, I'll turn it down.
2   A: ....   B: OK, I'll switch it on.
3   A: ....   B: OK, I'll take it off.
4   A: ....   B: OK, I'll throw them away.

c Practise the dialogues in **a** and **b** with a partner.

d Which of the verbs in **a** and **b** could you use with these nouns?

washing machine	stereo	TV	kettle	rubbish
money	clothes	computer	things	fire

Can you think of other possibilities?

e Give a partner some commands, using the verbs in **a**. Your partner should
carry out your instructions. For example:

'Take some money out of your pocket.'
'Hang your jacket up.'

'Tidy up my room? I have!!'

Answers

1 a They seem to be trying to raise money for something, possibly to build a swimming pool. Last night they had a meeting or money-raising event of some kind.

b
except for – apart from
to tell you the truth – to be honest
for some time – for quite a while
I guess so – I suppose so
generally speaking – on the whole
up to now – so far
by myself – on my own
that's a pity – what a shame
good luck – all the best

d The seven further changes are in italics in the tapescript below.

Tapescript

1 d Listen to the conversation and follow the instructions on your worksheet.

A: How many people turned up last night?
B: *Almost* everyone apart from Tom.
A: Oh, what happened to him?
B: *I haven't the faintest idea.* To be honest, I haven't seen him for quite a while, so I think he's more or less given up.
A: Well, that's a bit poor, isn't it? I mean he's going to benefit as much as *anybody* when it's *completed*.
B: Oh yes, he's *mad about swimming*. Still, we'll just have to manage without him.
A: I suppose so. How's it going, anyway?
B: Well, on the whole we're doing quite well. So far we've raised *nearly* four thousand and I'm hoping for another couple of hundred from my sponsored walk next week.
A: I thought Jill was doing that with you.
B: She was, but unfortunately *there's something wrong with* her back, so I'll have to do it on my own.
A: Oh, what a shame. Anyway, all the best – I hope it goes well.

Key words and expressions

Verbs	Prepositional phrases	Conversational expressions	Other words and expressions
give up	by myself	(a) couple of	apart from
turn up	for quite a while	all the best	except for
	for some time	good luck	generally speaking
	on my own	How's it going?	manage without
	on the whole	I guess so	so far
	up to now	I hope it goes well	sponsored walk
			I suppose so
			that's a bit poor
			that's a pity
			to be honest
			to tell you the truth
			what a shame

1 a **Read through the following dialogue. What are the two people talking about?**

A: How many people turned up last night?

B: Just about everyone *except for* Tom.

A: Oh, what happened to him?

B: I've no idea. *To tell you the truth,* I haven't seen him *for some time* so I think he's more or less given up.

A: Well, that's a bit poor, isn't it? I mean, he's going to benefit as much as anyone when it's finished.

B: Oh yes, he's a very keen swimmer. Still, we'll just have to manage without him.

A: *I guess so.* How's it going anyway?

B: Well, *generally speaking* we're doing quite well. *Up to now* we've raised almost four thousand, and I'm hoping for another couple of hundred from my sponsored walk next week.

A: I thought Jill was doing that with you.

B: She was, but unfortunately she's done something to her back, so I'll have to do it *by myself.*

A: Oh, *that's a pity.* Anyway, *good luck* – I hope it goes well.

b **Work with a partner. Look at the words and expressions in italics in the dialogue in a. Can you replace these parts of the dialogue with the following phrases?**

on the whole	apart from	so far	on my own	all the best
for quite a while	to be honest	what a shame	I suppose so	

c **Make seven more changes to the dialogue. The meaning must stay the same. Work with a partner and, when you have finished, read your dialogue to another pair. Discuss any changes which you think are incorrect.**

came

Example: A: How many people ~~turned up~~ last night?

d 🔲 **Listen to the dialogue from a. It includes the nine phrases from the box in b, and seven further changes. Mark the changes in your dialogue. Are they the same as those you made in c?**

Answers

1 a
in   business/advance/time
by   heart/mistake/choice/chance
on   strike/business/fire/time/foot

b **The probable answers are:**

1   … still on strike.
2   … took it by mistake.
3   … took it by choice.
4   … it by heart.
5   … met him by chance.
6   …'s gone on business.
7   …'s still on fire.
8   … got there on time.
9   … need to book in advance.

c **Some phrases you could elicit are:**

in control, in danger, in love
by accident, by hand, by post
on average, on holiday, on purpose

2 a
1   She's getting off the bus.
2   The plane has just taken off.
3   They are driving off / setting off in a car.
4   She's falling off her horse.
5   The handle has broken off / come off.
6   He's taking off his jacket.

b **In all the sentences *off* suggests 'separation' or 'leaving'.**

c **Here, too, the sentences have the idea of 'separation' or 'leaving'.**

Key words and expressions

Prepositional phrases	Verbs
by chance	be off (to)
by choice	break off
by heart	come off
by mistake	cut off
in advance	drive off
in time	fall off
on business	get off (a bus)
on fire	hurry off
on foot	see someone off
on strike	set off
on time	take off
	turn off

Phrases and phrasal verbs 10

Worksheet 3

1 a Many phrases in English are formed with a preposition and another word, usually a noun or a verb. How many different prepositional phrases can you find by combining the prepositions on the left with the nouns on the right? Use a dictionary to check your answers.

in	strike heart business fire advance
by	mistake time choice foot chance
on	

b Respond to the following questions, using a suitable prepositional phrase in your answer. When you have finished, practise the dialogues with a partner. For example:

A: Did you go by bus?
B: No, I went *on foot*.

1 A: Have they gone back to work?
   B: No, they're ....

2 A: Did you mean to take her coat?
   B: No, I ....

3 A: Did you have to take the exam?
   B: No, I ....

4 A: Did you give your speech from notes?
   B: No, I learnt ....

5 A: Were you planning to meet him?
   B: No, I ....

6 A: Is she there on holiday?
   B: No, she ....

7 A: Have the fire brigade put it out?
   B: No, it ....

8 A: Were you late for class this morning?
   B: No, I ....

9 A: Can you buy tickets on the night?
   B: No, you ....

c Can you think of any more prepositional phrases with *in, by* or *on*?

2 a Write a sentence including the word *off* to describe what is happening or what has just happened in the following pictures.

b What meaning (or meanings) does *off* have in the pictures in **a**?

c Look at the following sentences. Is the meaning of *off* the same as above or different?

1 When she saw me, she hurried off in the opposite direction.
2 When are you off to Switzerland?
3 We didn't pay the bill so they cut off our electricity.
4 I went to the airport to see them off.
5 Follow the main road and turn off just before you get to the motorway.
6 I'm going to take a few days off work next week.

PHOTOCOPIABLE © Cambridge University Press 1996   41

Answers

1 a This is a matter of opinion.

c These are the likely answers.

1 dishonest
2 lucky
3 generous
4 careless
5 stupid
6 wise/careful
7 lucky/clever
8 clever/wise

2 a *Hardly ever* is likely to be the only new item here, but you should remind students of the word order with these adverbs, i.e. before the verb, with the exception of the verb *to be*.

always
often
quite often
sometimes
occasionally
hardly ever
never

Key words and expressions

Nouns	Verbs	Adjectives	Other words and expressions
change	earn	careful	hardly ever
cheque	find	careless	occasionally
counterfoil	give (something) away	clever	(quite) often
credit card	inherit	dishonest	sometimes
purse	invest	generous	
wallet	lend	lucky	
	lose	stupid	
	save	wise	
	spend		
	steal		
	tip		
	waste		
	win		

1 a There are lots of different ways you can get money. Here are five:

earn it   steal it   win it   inherit it   find it

Which are the most common? Put them in order, then compare with a partner.

b There are also lots of things you can do with money. Here are six:

lose it   spend it   give it away   invest it   save it   waste it

Of these six, which give you the most pleasure and happiness? Put them in order. Compare your answers with your partner's.

c Complete the sentences below with adjectives from the box (or any others you would like to use).

| stupid   generous   lucky   dishonest   careless   careful   wise   clever |

1 Someone who steals a lot is ....
2 Someone who inherits money is ....
3 Someone who gives their money away is ....
4 Someone who often loses money is ....
5 Someone who wastes their money is ....
6 Someone who saves most of their money is ....
7 Someone who earns a lot of money is ....
8 Someone who invests most of their money is ....

2 a Put the words in the box on the scale below.

| hardly ever   occasionally   often   sometimes   quite often |

always
        ....
            ....
                ....
                    ....
                        ....
                            never

'Do we accept cash?'

b In pairs, ask each other the questions below. Try to use the words from **a** in your answers. For example:

You: Do you lose money?
Your partner: Hardly ever.

1 Do you ever find money?
2 Do you give money to strangers in the street if they ask you for money?
3 Do you carry a lot of money on you when you go out?
4 Do you pay for things with a credit card?
5 Do you fill in the counterfoil when you write a cheque?
6 Do you tip waiters?
7 Do you keep your money in a wallet or a purse?
8 Do you keep a record of the money you spend?
9 Do you check your change in shops?
10 Do you lend money to friends?

c Which of your partner's answers were surprising?

© Cambridge University Press 1996

Answers

1 a
1 How much did that watch cost (you)?
2 Could I borrow a pen?
3 I'm afraid I can't afford that car.
4 I earn about £15,000 a year.
5 Some friends are going to rent his house.
6 This picture is worth a lot of money.

2 a

Shopping	*£*
computer	360
clothes	97
coffee maker	35
decanter and glasses	60
presents for family	224 *(half of £448)*
cassettes	66
painting	40
lunch and taxi	15
total spent	897

She ended up with £103.

b

		Problem?	*What happened?*
1	decanter and glasses	two cracked glasses	got a credit note
2	coffee maker	electrical fault	threw it away
3	scarf	–	lost it
4	computer	couldn't get used to it	sold it to her brother

Tapescript

2 b **Listen to the conversation and follow the instructions on your worksheet.**

M: This afternoon, I thought I'd get a few things in the sales.
W: Well, be careful. I bought loads of things in the January sales and some of them turned out to be a bit of a disaster.
M: Oh yeah?
W: Yeah. I got a decanter and a set of wine glasses, and when I got home and unpacked them, I discovered that two of them had a little crack in them.
M: Did you take them back?
W: Yeah, but you can't get your money back on sale goods; all I got was a credit note, which wasn't much use as there was nothing else I wanted to buy.
M: Yeah, that's always the way.
W: And do you remember that coffee maker I told you about?
M: Er, yeah, I think so.
W: Well, *that* never worked properly; there was something wrong with the electrics and in the end I threw it away.
M: Oh, what a shame.
W: Well, I suppose that's the risk you take. I got a lovely jacket and skirt and I wear *them* all the time. Unfortunately, I lost the scarf I got to go with them, but never mind. Oh … and the oil painting I got is really one of my favourite things.
M: The one beside the bookcase in the living room?
W: Yeah. I got that in a sale. I love it – wish I could say the same about that computer; couldn't get the hang of it at all. I sold it to my brother in the end.
M: Really? I've been thinking of getting a computer for ages.
W: You could look for one in the sales. You might get one really cheaply.

Key words and expressions

Nouns	Verbs	Adjectives	Other words and expressions
coffee maker	(can't) afford	expensive	be worth
decanter	borrow	valuable	for ages
dozen	cost		have (£5) left
fare	get money off		I almost forgot to mention
oil painting	lend		(10 per cent /£5) off
retail price	let (a house)		reduced from (£9) to (£7)
salary	pay (£5) for something		set (of wine glasses)
sale	rent		spending spree
tip	spend money on		

Money 11

1 a Rewrite the following sentences, using one of the words below for each sentence. The meanings of the sentences must remain the same. Use your dictionary to look up any new words, and look carefully at any example sentences in your dictionary; they will help you with the grammatical constructions you will need.

> borrow   afford   rent   worth   earn   sell   cost

Example: I bought it from John. ..John..sold..it..to..me.....................

1   How much did you pay for that watch?
   ....

2   Could you lend me a pen?
   ....

3   I'm afraid that car is too expensive for me.
   ....

4   My salary is about £15,000 a year.
   ....

5   He's going to let his house to some friends.
   ....

6   This picture is very valuable.
   ....

b Now make questions using the verbs in **a**. Each question must have a *Yes* or *No* answer. Go round the class asking your questions and continue until you get a *Yes* answer to each question.

Example: 'Please can I borrow your dictionary?'

2 a Joanna went shopping with £1,000. Read the text and then answer this question: from the original £1,000 how much money did Joanna have left?

First of all she bought herself a computer as she'd wanted one for ages. The retail price was £400 but, as she bought it in a sale, she got 10% off. After that she went to a boutique where she got a jacket and matching skirt for £85 and a silk scarf, which cost her £12. In another sale she got a very smart coffee maker reduced from £45 to £35, plus a decanter and set of six wine glasses for 25% less than the normal price of £80. Half of what she had left went on presents for her family, and she then finished her spending spree with half a dozen music cassettes at £11 each, and a small oil painting. The man in the shop wanted £50 for the painting but she persuaded him to sell it for £40. Oh yes, I almost forgot to mention £5 that she spent on lunch; and the taxi fare home, which cost her another £10 including the tip.

b [cassette icon] Listen to Joanna talking about the things she bought and fill in the table.

		Problem?	*What happened?*
1	decanter and glasses		
2	coffee maker		
3	scarf		
4	computer		

Answers

1 a
2 'The Great White Hope'.
3 Howard Sackler.
4 At the Mermaid Theatre.
5 Hugh Quarshire.
6 Nicolas Kent.
7 Boxing.
8 It sounds very good, but I don't know until I see it.

c Questions you can use about a book: 2, 3, 7, 8
Questions you can use about a film: 1, 2, 4, 5, 6, 7, 8
Questions you can use about a TV programme: 2, 5, 6, 7, 8

d **When students have decided upon appropriate questions for a book, film and TV programme, put them into pairs to interview each other on an example of their choice. For example:**

– Have you read *David Copperfield*? (What's it like/about?)
– Have you seen *The Last Emperor*? (Where's it on? Who's in it?)

Tapescript

1 b **Listen to the questions and answers.**

1 A: Is there anything on at the moment?
   B: There's a new play starting next week.

2 A: What's it called?
   B: 'The Great White Hope'.

3 A: Who's it by?
   B: Howard Sackler.

4 A: Where's it on?
   B: At the Mermaid Theatre.

5 A: Who's in it?
   B: Hugh Quarshire.

6 A: Who's it directed by?
   B: Nicolas Kent.

7 A: What's it about?
   B: Boxing.

8 A: What's it like?
   B: It sounds very good, but I don't know until I see it.

Key words and expressions

Nouns
play

Other expressions
Is there (anything) on?
What's (it) about?
What's (it) called?
What's (it) like?
Where's (it) on?
Who's (it) by?
Who's (it) directed by?
Who's in (it)?

1 a Here are some common questions which you should learn as complete phrases. Look at the advertisement. How many of the questions can you answer?

1 Is there anything on at the moment?
There's a new play starting next week.

2 What's it called?
....

3 Who's it by?
....

4 Where's it on?
....

5 Who's in it?
....

6 Who's it directed by?
....

7 What's it about?
....

8 What's it like?
....

THE AWARD WINNING PRODUCTION OF

THE GREAT WHITE HOPE

BY HOWARD SACKLER

'Crowning this evening is Hugh Quarshire... an irresistibly convincing performance as the first black heavyweight champion' LISTENER

'Brilliantly directed' by Nicolas Kent D. TELEGRAPH

OPENS THIS WEEK
Reduced price previews
13-20 August

ADVANCED BOOKING
0171 236 5568, 638 8891, 741 9999(INCL SUN)

MERMAID THEATRE
PUDDLE DOCK LONDON EC4

TWO MAJOR
THEATRE AWARDS IN 1986

b 🖭 Listen to the same questions and answers on the cassette, and notice how the words are joined together.

Example: What's‿it called?

c How many of the questions can you use to ask about a book, a film or a TV programme?

d Have you been to the theatre or cinema recently? Have you read any books? Have you seen any films on TV? Tell a partner, and use phrases from **a** where suitable.

Answers

1 a

Job	Place	Duties
vet	surgery	treats sick animals
stockbroker	stock exchange	buys and sells stocks and shares
firefighter	fire station	fights/puts out fires
priest/vicar	church	performs religious ceremonies and helps people in the community
dustman	in the streets	collects people's rubbish
surgeon	hospital	operates on people
plumber	any building	installs/fixes water pipes and appliances
miner	mine	mines coal/silver/diamonds, etc.
journalist	office/anywhere	writes newspaper (or magazine) reports (or works on TV/radio news)
librarian	library	organises books and deals with lending of books
pilot	aeroplane cockpit	flies a plane
mechanic	garage	repairs/fixes cars
secretary	office	does general office work

b Begin by illustrating the pattern. For example:

A: What do you call a person who flies a plane?
B: A pilot.

Students can then practise in pairs.

Key words and expressions

Nouns	Verbs	Adjectives	Other expressions
architect	buy	exciting	anti-social hours
cockpit	collect	qualified	early retirement
church	design	stressful	high status
dustman	fight	well-organised	
firefighter	fix	well paid	
fire station	fly		
garage	install		
hospital	mine		
journalist	operate		
librarian	organise		
library	perform		
mechanic	put out		
mine	repair		
miner	sell		
plumber	treat		
pilot	write		
priest			
secretary			
stockbroker			
stock exchange			
street			
surgeon			
surgery			
vet			
vicar			

1 a Complete the chart below.

Job	Place	Duties
architect	office	designs buildings
		treats sick animals
	stock exchange	
firefighter		
	church	
dustman		
		operates on people
plumber		
	mine	
		writes newspaper reports
	library	
pilot		
	garage	
secretary		

b Now define the duties of a particular job and see if a partner can guess the job. Use the jobs in a and any others you know. For example:

A: What do you call a person who designs houses?
B: An architect.

c Now compile your own chart of the good and bad points of these jobs. Work with your partner and use a dictionary to help you. For example:

Job	Good points	Bad points
pilot	well paid, exciting, high status	anti-social hours, stressful, early retirement

Librarian
Walton Public Library is looking for a LIBRARIAN. We need a professionally qualified librarian with experience in a local library. An ability to use computers is an advantage. Please write to: Mrs J. Smith, Walton Public Library, The High Street, Walton, Cambridge.

Secretary
SECRETARY needed in a busy London office.
• Can you type?
• Are you well-organised?
• Have you got five or more passes at GSCE? If you can answer yes to these questions, phone 0171 123 4567 for more details.

Journalist
JOURNALIST An exciting opportunity for a person with journalistic experience to work on a well-known national newspaper. Please fax your CV to 0171 321 4567.

Plumber
PLUMBER WANTED. 20 hours per week. Good salary. Please phone John on 01223 91119.

Vet
Broadtown Surgery is looking for a vet to work with dogs and cats. The ideal candidate will have at least three years experience working with small animals. For further details tel: 0151 32467.

Mechanic
MECHANIC wanted in busy garage. Phone Bob on 01975 753753.

Answers

1 a Here is the probable order:

1 She saw the advert.
2 She applied for the job.
3 They gave her an interview.
4 They offered her the job.
5 She accepted the job.
6 She got promotion.
7 They weren't satisfied with her work.
8 They sacked her.

b The facts about the two jobs are as follows (and students could have selected any four from each list):

Present job	*New job*
in charge of a small team	contact with engineers, builders, etc.
a lot of responsibility	a lot of travelling locally
desk job/paperwork	a lower salary
little chance of promotion	good promotion prospects
a small company	part of a new project

2 a The best answer is:

type of organisation	multinational
career prospects	rapid promotion
salary	£30,000
location	on the outskirts of Manchester
responsibilities	in charge of a small department
job satisfaction	demanding but stimulating
fringe benefits	company car and petrol allowance
work environment	comfortable and spacious offices

Tapescript

1 b Listen to the interview and follow the instructions on your worksheet.

M: Well, now then, one thing I'd like to ask is, er, exactly why you applied for the job. I mean, just looking at your application form, you're actually overqualified …

W: Yes, I thought you might ask that. Um, the thing is, in my present job, although I'm actually in charge of a small team and I have a lot of responsibility, it's largely a desk job with a lot of paperwork …

M: And you're not too keen on being stuck in an office all day?

W: To be honest, no, I'm not. I much prefer being out on site where I can supervise things, and deal with problems as they occur. And this job should give me that kind of contact with other engineers, architects, builders and so on.

M: Mmm. You'd certainly have to do quite a lot of travelling in the local area, you know, visiting different sites. You do realise, though, that the starting salary isn't as good as the salary in your present job?

W: Yes, I realise that, but um, it does say in the job advertisement that the promotion prospects are very good.

M: That's true, and er, as this is a new project that we're working on, we think there'll be a very good chance of fairly quick promotion, depending on performance, that is …

W: Yes, of course. Well, you see, I've got very little chance of promotion in my present job. I mean it's a very small company and there's nowhere really for me to go; that's why I'm looking around for somewhere else.

Key words and expressions

Nouns			Verbs	Adjectives	Other expressions
advert (advertisement)	fringe benefits	responsibility	accept	demanding	be satisfied with
application form	interview	salary	apply for (a job)	spacious	be stuck in (a place)
architect	job satisfaction	work environment	sack	stimulating	get promotion
builder	location				give (someone) an interview
career prospects	paperwork				offer (someone) a job
company car	petrol allowance				starting salary
engineer	promotion				

1 a Read the sentences below about Sarah's last job. With a partner, put them into the order in which you think they occurred.

She accepted the job.	....
She saw the advert.	....
She got promotion.	....
She applied for the job.	....
They weren't satisfied with her work.	....
They gave her an interview.	....
They sacked her.	....
They offered her the job.	....

b 🔲 Listen to the interview. Write down four facts about Sarah's present job, and four facts about the new job she is applying for. Use the table below for your answers.

	Present job	New job
1		
2		
3		
4		

'I've told you about the pay, holidays, pension, sick pay, perks and free lunches . . . wouldn't you like to know what the job is?'

2 a Match the job factors in column A with the examples in column B.

A	B
type of organisation	on the outskirts of Manchester
career prospects	demanding but stimulating
salary	multinational
location	£30,000
responsibilities	comfortable and spacious offices
job satisfaction	company car and petrol allowance
fringe benefits	in charge of a small department
work environment	rapid promotion

b Rank the job factors in column A in order of importance to you personally and then compare your answers in groups.

Answers

1 a

departure lounge	boarding card
holiday resort	traveller's cheques
excess baggage	passport control
suitcase	runway
charter flight	take-off
duty-free	check-in desk
travel agency	seat belt

b First of all, we went to a *travel agency* to get some information. We decided to go to a *holiday resort* abroad and we managed to get a *charter flight*, which saved us some money. Later we went to the bank and got some *traveller's cheques*. At the airport we took our *suitcases* to the *check-in* desk. They were quite heavy but we didn't have to pay *excess baggage*. Then we went through *passport control* and waited for about half an hour in the *departure lounge*. While we waited, we looked round the *duty-free* and bought some sunglasses. When they called our flight, we got on the plane and showed the stewardess our *boarding cards*. We found our seats and fastened our *seat belts*. Then we taxied to the *runway* and waited for *take-off*.

2 a

2	big	7	bad
3	nice/good	8	dirty
4	small	9	old
5	tired	10	good
6	cold		

b

1	Yeah, it was really big.	4	Yeah, it was very old.
2	Yeah, it was very dirty.	5	Yeah, it was really bad.
3	Yeah, it was really small.	6	Yeah, we were very tired.

c

1	ancient	5	filthy
2	tiny	6	freezing
3	delicious	7	boiling
4	awful	8	exhausted

Tapescript

2 b Listen to these examples.

A: It was freezing, wasn't it?
B: Yeah, it was very cold.

A: Delicious food, wasn't it?
B: Yeah, it was really good.

Now listen and reply.

1 A: It was enormous, wasn't it?
2 A: It was filthy, wasn't it?
3 A: Oh, the flat was tiny, wasn't it?
4 A: And it was ancient, wasn't it?
5 A: Oh, it was an awful journey, wasn't it?
6 A: And we were exhausted, weren't we?

Key words and expressions

Nouns		**Adjectives**	**Other words and expressions**
boarding card	runway	ancient	go abroad
charter flight	seat belt	awful	
check-in desk	stewardess	boiling	
departure lounge	suitcase	delicious	
duty-free	take-off	enormous	
excess baggage	travel agency	exhausted	
holiday resort	traveller's cheques	filthy	
information		freezing	
passport control		tiny	
		wonderful	

1 a Match the words in box A with the words in box B to form new nouns.

Example: departure lounge

A	B
departure holiday excess suit charter duty travel boarding traveller's passport run take check-in seat	agency card control off belt flight desk lounge way free baggage resort cheques case

'Duty-free' does not mean without responsibility, sir...

hic

b Now use the words and phrases from **a** to complete the story below. The first one has been done for you.

First of all, we went to a ...*travel agency*... to get some information. We decided to go to a .... abroad and we managed to get a ...., which saved us some money. Later we went to the bank and got some .... At the airport we took our .... to the .... desk. They were quite heavy but we didn't have to pay .... Then we went through .... and waited for about half an hour in the .... While we waited, we looked round the .... and bought some sunglasses. When they called our flight, we got on the plane and showed the stewardess our .... We found our seats and fastened our .... Then we taxied to the .... and waited for ....

2 a Complete the table below with a suitable *normal* adjective for each *extreme* one.

	Normal	Extreme		Normal	Extreme
1	hot	boiling	6		freezing
2		enormous	7		awful
3		delicious	8		filthy
4		tiny	9		ancient
5		exhausted	10		wonderful

b 🔊 Listen to these example conversations:

A: It was freezing, wasn't it?　　　A: Delicious food, wasn't it?
B: Yeah, it was very cold.　　　　　B: Yeah, it was really good.

You will now hear some questions. Can you reply to each of the questions as in the examples above?

c Put the extreme adjectives into the following conversation. (Ted and Edna always agree with each other!) For example:

Ted says …　　　　　　　　　　　　… and Edna replies …

It was a big hotel, wasn't it?　　　　Yes, it was ..*enormous*.........................

1	But it wasn't very modern, was it?	No, it was ....
2	And the room wasn't very big either.	No, it was ....
3	But the food was nice.	It was ....
4	I didn't like the coffee, though.	No, it was ....
5	The beach wasn't very clean, I thought.	No, it was ....
6	And the sea wasn't very warm.	No, it was ....
7	Still, we had lovely weather.	Yes, it was ....
8	Are you tired after the flight?	Oh yes, I'm ....

Answers

1 a If students find this part very easy, you could expand the new input by asking them to think of three more words to describe each place. With the existing words, though, you will need to check the pronunciation of *yacht* /jɒt/ and *sunbathe* /sʌnbeɪð/.

1 The beach scene: beach, sand, coastline, steep, cliffs, tourists, steps, overlooking, sunbathe, view
2 The harbour scene: harbour, yachts, tourists, hectic, view, rocks
3 The mountain scene: valley, mountains, lake, countryside, snow, peaceful, remote, surrounded by, in the distance, steep, view

b Students often confuse *touristic* ('related to tourists') with *touristy* ('full of tourists'). The latter is usually used to show disapproval.

	Noun	Adjective
1	sand	sandy
2	rocks	rocky
3	mountain	mountainous
4	tourist	touristy

c Sample answers

1 This is a picture of where we are staying. We are in one of the hotels overlooking the beach and we have a great view of the coastline and cliffs. Every day we go down to the beach and sunbathe. It only takes us two minutes to get there down some steep steps. We are really relaxing: it is very quiet as there aren't many other tourists here. See you soon.

2 This is the harbour in the town where we are staying. It is really pretty, with lots of yachts and boats. Our hotel isn't in the picture, but we have a good view of the harbour. There are lots of tourists from the yachts so life is quite hectic! Lots of people walking around and a lot of cars. It's fun!

3 Well, here we are, in the peace and quiet of the countryside at last. It's a very remote and peaceful place. As you can see, the lake is surrounded by steep mountains with snow on them, and in the distance we can see a little valley. We are staying quite near this lake and we have a marvellous view from our hotel. We don't want to come home!

Key words and expressions

Nouns	Adjectives	Verbs	Other words and expressions
beach	hectic	sunbathe	in the distance
cliff	mountainous		surrounded by
coastline	overlooking		
countryside	peaceful		
harbour	remote		
lake	rocky		
mountain	sandy		
rocks	snowy		
sand	steep		
snow	touristy		
step			
tourist			
valley			
view			
yacht			

1 a Look at these three places and then study the words and phrases in the box. Which words and phrases would you need to describe each place? (You can use a word or phrase to describe more than one place.)

> valley mountains yachts beach
> countryside coastline cliffs remote
> steep hectic steps lake view
> in the distance rocks sand snow
> harbour surrounded by tourists
> sunbathe (v) peaceful overlooking

b You may also want to use the adjectives formed from some of the nouns above. What are the adjectives formed from these nouns?

Noun	Adjective
sand	....
rocks	....
mountain	....
tourist	....

c Imagine you are staying in one of these three places. Write a postcard describing the place and your holiday, using the words you selected in **a**. Then give your postcard to someone in your class and ask them to guess which place you are writing from.

Answers

1 b
a close friend
a hard worker
a strong accent
a big disappointment
a serious illness
a high salary
a light sleeper/smoker
a heavy smoker/sleeper

2 a **These are the probable combinations:**

a hot or mild curry
sweet or dry wine
strong or weak tea
a rough or calm sea
a hard or soft bed
hot or cold water
sweet or sour grapes
strong or mild cheese/cigarettes
a rough or smooth surface/skin
a hard or easy exam

Key words and expressions

Adjectives and nouns

big disappointment
calm sea
close friend
cold water
dry wine
easy exam
hard bed
hard skin
hard worker
heavy rain
heavy sleeper
heavy smoker
high salary
hot curry
hot water
light sleeper
light smoker
mild cheese
mild cigarettes

mild curry
rough sea
rough skin
rough surface
serious illness
smooth skin
smooth surface
soft bed
soft skin
sour grapes
strong accent
strong cheese
strong cigarettes
strong tea
strong wind
sweet orange
sweet wine
weak tea

Other expressions

do one's homework
make a mistake

Collocation 15

1 a We often combine words in certain ways. In English, for example, we can say:

heavy rain   a strong wind   make a mistake   do one's homework

Other languages may use different adjectives or verbs with these nouns. It is important, therefore, to learn the different partners that words can have. This worksheet looks at some common examples.

b Which adjectives in box A can you combine with the nouns in box B?

A		B	
close	serious	sleeper	salary
hard	high	disappointment	worker
strong	light	friend	accent
big	heavy	illness	smoker

c Complete the sentences with adjectives from **b**. Then move round the class and ask questions to complete the chart.

Find someone who ...	Name
... is a .... sleeper.	_____
... is a .... smoker.	_____
... is a .... worker.	_____
... has (or will have) a .... salary.	_____
... doesn't think they have a .... foreign accent when they speak English.	_____
... has had a .... illness in their life.	_____
... has recently had a .... disappointment.	_____
... has a .... friend of a different nationality.	_____

2 a Which of the pairs of adjectives on the left can you use with the nouns on the right?

hot or mild	hot or cold	sea	cheese
sweet or dry	sweet or sour	curry	bed
strong or weak	strong or mild	water	wine
rough or calm	rough or smooth	cigarettes	tea
hard or soft	hard or easy	exam	grapes
		skin	surface

b Now practise these combinations by contradicting your partner like this:

Your partner: This cheese is strong.
You: Do you think so? I thought it was quite mild.

57

Answers

1 **We say:**

do the shopping
do the washing-up
do the cooking
make the bed(s)
do the cleaning
make the most money
make the most mess
do the ironing
make most of the decisions

2 **a** 1 a cheque: anyone, in a shop, to pay for something
an article: a journalist, in an office, it's his/her job
an essay: a student, in a library, the teacher wants it
a novel: a novelist, at home, for pleasure or money

2 tyres and brakes: a mechanic, in a garage, for safety
passports: passport officer, at the airport, for security
answers: a teacher, in class, to see if you understand
their change: anyone, in a shop, to see that it's right

3 an application form: anyone, at home, to apply for a job
gaps: a student, in a test, to try and pass the test
a questionnaire: anyone, in the street, someone asked them to
a counterfoil: anyone, in a shop, to remember what you have paid and where

Key words and expressions

Nouns	Other expressions
answer	do the cleaning
application form	do the cooking
article	do the ironing
brakes	do the shopping
change	do the washing-up
cheque	make the bed(s)
counterfoil	make a decision
essay	make a mess
gap	make money
novel	
novelist	
passport	
questionnaire	
tyre	

Collocation 15

1 **In your house, who *does* or *makes* things? Complete the chart with:**

— the correct verb *do* or *make*
— the person who does each thing in your house (write a tick)

Do or make?		*A man*	*A woman*	*Either*
	the shopping	✓✓	✓	✓
	the washing-up			
	the cooking			
	the bed(s)			
	the cleaning			
	the most money			
	the most mess			
	the ironing			
	most of the decisions			

Now ask the other people in your group who does these things in their homes. (Mark their answers with ticks.) What can you say about the results of your survey?

* Exercise 1 is taken from *Working with Words* by Ruth Gairns and Stuart Redman, Cambridge University Press, 1986.

2 a **Look at the following table and fill it in. Your answers may be very general e.g. *anyone*, or very specific e.g. *a journalist*.**

			Who?	*Where?*	*Why?*
1	writes	a cheque	anyone	in a shop	to pay for something
		an article			
		an essay			
		a novel			
2	checks	tyres and brakes			
		passports			
		answers			
		their change			
3	fills in	an application form			
		gaps			
		a questionnaire			
		a counterfoil			

b **Now compare your answers with a partner's.**

Answers

1 a **Some possible spoken questions are:**

What's your surname / family name?
What's your first name?
When were you born?
Where do you come from? / Where are you from?
What do you do (for a living)? / What's your job/occupation?
Are you married (single or divorced)?
Where do you live?
Where are you living / staying at the moment / at present?
Why are you here? / Why have you come here? / What are you here for?
How long are you staying? / How long do you intend to stay?

b Surname: Bajan
Forename: Sonia
Date of birth: 3 February 1972
Country of origin: Switzerland
Occupation: Bank employee
Marital status: Married

Permanent address: Richttanne, 8627 Gruningen
Temporary address: 18 Brackley Road, London W4
Purpose of visit: General language course
Length of stay: Five and a half months
Date: 13th ......

c **See tapescript below.**

Tapescript

1 b **Listen to the interview and follow the instructions on your worksheet.**

W: Right. If I could just ask you a few questions? Um, let's start with your name.
S: It's Sonia.
W: Sonia. OK. And your family name?
S: Bajan.
W: Bajan. How do you spell that?
S: B-A-J-A-N.
W: Right. OK. And where are you from, Sonia?
S: From Switzerland.
W: Switzerland.
S: Yes.
W: Bajan's not a very Swiss name, is it?
S: No, it isn't. It's Hungarian.
W: Hungarian? Really?
S: Yes.
W: Is your family Hungarian?
S: No. It's my husband's family.
W: Oh, I see. So you're married then?
S: Yes.
W: OK. And what do you do in Switzerland?

S: I work in a bank.
W: In a bank. Right. And whereabouts do you live in Switzerland?
S: Near Zurich.
W: Near Zurich. OK. Er, what's the address?
S: It's Richttanne.
W: Could you spell that please?
S: Yes. R-I-C-H-double T-A-double N-E.
W: Thanks.
S: And then it's 8627 Gruningen.
W: Gruningen. I've heard that before; I know that. OK. Right. And where are you staying here in England?
S: In London.
W: Right. With a family?
S: Yes.
W: OK. What's the address?
S: 18 Brackley Road.
W: Brackley?
S: Yes, Brackley Road.
W: Yeah.
S: W4. London W4.

W: Fine. OK. And what are you here for exactly?
S: Oh, I'm doing a general language course.
W: In a, in a language school?
S: Yes.
W: I see. Your English sounds pretty good to me. And er, how long, how long will you be here for?
S: Five and a half months.
W: That's quite a long time. That's nice.
S: Yeah.
W: And um when were you born?
S: February the 3rd, 1972.
W: OK. I think that's about all. Um, could you just sign here for me, please?
S: Yeah, sure.
W: And write the date here.
S: Is it the thirteenth?
W: Yeah, the thirteenth. OK, that's it. Lovely. Thanks very much.

Key words and expressions

Nouns		Verbs	Adjectives	Other words and expressions	
advertisement	occupation	fill in (a form)	medical	country of origin	Are you married?
(birth) certificate	surname	open (an account)	permanent	date of birth	How long are you staying?
credit card	traveller's cheques	register	temporary	international	What do you do?
examination	vaccination	sign		driving licence	What's your name?
forename	visa			length of visit	When were you born?
form	work permit			marital status	Where are you from?
injection				permanent address	Where do you live?
insurance				purpose of visit	Why are you here?
				temporary address	

1 a The following form is written in formal English. In spoken English we might ask for this information in a different way. For example:

Country of origin – 'Where are you from?' or 'Where do you come from?'

Now do the same for the rest of the form: in spoken English what questions would you ask to get each piece of information? (Do not fill in the form yet.)

SURNAME:	FORENAME:	DATE OF BIRTH:
COUNTRY OF ORIGIN:	OCCUPATION:	MARITAL STATUS:
PERMANENT ADDRESS:	TEMPORARY ADDRESS:	
PURPOSE OF VISIT:	LENGTH OF VISIT:	
	SIGNED:	
	DATE:	

b 🔲 Listen to the interview and fill in the form in **a**.

c 🔲 Listen to the interview a second time. Does the interviewer use the same question forms as you did? If not, write down the question forms she uses.

d Imagine you are an official and your partner is someone who has just arrived in Britain. Practise the conversation.

2 a Alison Cook has decided to live and work in your country for one year. Look at the three columns below. Next to each item put 'N' for necessary, or 'A' for advisable, or 'U' for unnecessary, or 'I' for impossible. Work with your partner and use a dictionary if necessary.

Before leaving England	*When she arrives*	*Essential documents to take*
have lessons to learn your language	get a work permit	passport
have injections	register with the police	birth certificate
get a visa	register with the British Embassy	credit cards
buy traveller's cheques	open a bank account	British driving licence
take out medical insurance	get a permanent address (not a hotel)	examination certificates
take out travel insurance	look at job advertisements in the local paper	vaccination certificates
get an international driving licence		international driving licence

b Is there any more advice you could give Alison? Discuss your answers in groups.

Answers

1 a When you go through the answers, check the pronunciation of *brooch* /brəʊtʃ/, *bracelet* /breɪslət/, *necklace* /nekləs/, *tie* /taɪ/, and *gloves* /glʌvz/.

earrings: ears
gloves: hands
socks: feet
tie: neck
belt: waist
ring: finger
bracelet: wrist
cap: head
brooch: chest
hat: head
boots: feet
necklace: neck and shoulders
scarf: neck

2 a Tell students to use each item of vocabulary at least once. With a multilingual class it is advisable to bring something *suede* and *silk* into the class, otherwise these words will be very difficult to explain. If you work in a very hot climate or very cold climate, you may wish to change some of the vocabulary in order to make it more relevant to your students. In this case, write the items on the board.

There are a lot of possible answers. Here are some of them:

a thin cotton blouse
a long silk scarf
warm leather gloves
a thick suede jacket

Key words and expressions

Nouns

		Adjectives
belt	overcoat	-sleeved
blouse	ring	thick
boots	scarf	thin
bracelet	shoulder	warm
brooch	silk	woollen
cap	silver	
chest	skirt	
cotton	socks	
earrings	suede	
finger	tie	
gloves	trousers	
gold	T-shirt	
hat	waist	
jacket	wrist	
leather		
neck		
necklace		

Clothes and shopping 17

1 a Match the clothes and accessories on the left with the correct part of the body on the right.

earrings — waist
gloves — wrist
socks — hands
tie — ears
belt — finger
ring — feet
bracelet — neck
cap — head
brooch — chest
hat — neck and shoulders
boots
necklace
scarf

b Who is wearing what? Count the number of people in the class who are wearing these items.

2 a Combine the following words in different ways. For example:

thick woollen trousers

a	thick thin warm long short	-sleeved woollen cotton silk leather suede silver gold	overcoat jacket tie earrings skirt blouse scarf belt trousers necklace gloves T-shirt boots socks

b Who would wear these clothes? When would they wear them? For example: Someone on a beach might wear a thin cotton T-shirt.

c Work with a partner. Describe your partner's clothes using the adjectives in the table above.

d Describe the clothes of someone in your class, using the same adjectives. Do not mention the person's name. The other students should try to guess who you are describing.

Answers

1 a 1 Shop assistant: Can I help you?
Customer: I'm being served, thanks.

2 Customer: Excuse me. Have you got this blouse in size 12?
Shop assistant: No, I'm afraid we've sold out.
Customer: Oh, what a pity.

3 Customer: Could I try on this dress?
Shop assistant: Yes, of course. The changing-room's over there.
Customer: (*A few minutes later*) I'm afraid it's too small.
Shop assistant: Well, would you like to try on a bigger size?
Customer: Yes, please.

2 a **You can start on the 5th floor or in the basement:**

5th floor: a bed
4th floor: a cassette, a novel, a notepad
3rd floor: a tracksuit, an exercise bike, some underwear
2nd floor: some underwear
1st floor: two single sheets
ground floor: a tube of toothpaste, needles and thread
basement: a kettle, knives and forks

The present for Ted could be from any department.

b **The additional things were:**

a couple of other books
some envelopes
some toys (Jean bought these.)

Tapescript

2 b **Listen to Bob talking about his visit to the department store and answer the questions on your worksheet.**

Bob: Well, I went with Jean, my wife, and first of all we went straight to the furniture department on the top floor and ordered a bed. Then we went down a floor so Jean could go to the audio department and get a cassette she wanted. So I left her there while I bought a, a novel and a couple of other books – I thought one of them would make a nice present for Ted – and just next door I got a notepad and some envelopes at the same time.

Anyway, I went back and found Jean buying more toys for our two nephews so I quickly dragged her away and headed for the lift to take us to the sportswear department; I wanted to buy a tracksuit for jogging and have a look at some exercise bikes as well. Jean wasn't very interested so she went on down to the ladieswear department to look at some clothes. We met up again in the bedding department because we had to get some sheets, and then … er, went

back down to the ground floor where I got some toothpaste in toiletries and er, Jean went and bought some needles and thread.

Anyway, we finished up in the basement; we bought a kettle and some knives and forks and, er, oh, one or two things and as we were there we decided to have a cup of coffee. That was when I suddenly remembered I forgot to buy underwear when I was up in the menswear department.

Key words and expressions

Nouns		Verbs	Other words and expressions	
changing-room	furniture	try on	I'm afraid …	sold out
customer	kettle		I'm being served, thanks.	What a pity
department store	knife (pl. knives)		in size (12)	
envelope	needle and thread		in the basement	
folk music	notepad		on the first/second/top floor	
fork			over there	

1 a Make three short conversations from these mixed-up sentences. The three conversations are all between a shop assistant and a customer.

No, I'm afraid we've sold out. ......

Well, would you like to try on a bigger size? ......

Could I try on this dress? ......

I'm being served, thanks. ......

Oh, what a pity. ......

(*a few minutes later*) I'm afraid it's too small. ......

Yes, please. ......

Yes, of course. The changing-room's over there. ......

Can I help you? ......

Excuse me. Have you got this blouse in size 12? ......

b Now move round the class, practising similar conversations with different people.

2 a You are going to a large department store to do some shopping. Here is your list. Can you put the list in the best order to save time while you are shopping? The store directory will help you.

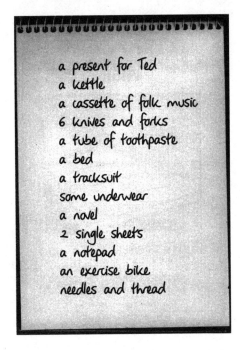

a present for Ted
a kettle
a cassette of folk music
6 knives and forks
a tube of toothpaste
a bed
a tracksuit
some underwear
a novel
2 single sheets
a notepad
an exercise bike
needles and thread

▶ **5th FLOOR:**
Furniture
▶ **4th FLOOR:**
Audio, Books, Stationery, Toys
▶ **3rd FLOOR:**
Menswear, Childrenswear, Sportswear and Sports Equipment
▶ **2nd FLOOR:**
Ladieswear and Lingerie
▶ **1st FLOOR:**
Towels and Linen, Bedding, Sewing Machines, Curtains
▶ **GROUND FLOOR:**
Toiletries, Haberdashery, Fabrics, Jewellery, Hats and Gloves, Tobacco, Confectionery
▶ **BASEMENT:**
China and Glass, Kitchenware, Cutlery, Electrical Appliances, Lighting, Gardening, Luggage, Coffee Shop

b Listen to the recording about Bob's visit to the department store. Is the order the same as yours? What *additional* things did Bob and his wife buy?

Answers

1 a
3   son
4   daughter-in-law
8   uncle
9   niece
10   aunt
12   grandfather
13   granddaughter
15   cousin
17   sister-in-law

Key words

Nouns
aunt
brother-in-law
cousin
daughter-in-law
father-in-law
granddaughter
grandfather
grandmother
grandson
mother-in-law
nephew
niece
sister-in-law
son-in-law
uncle
widow
widower

People and relationships

18

1 a Look at the family tree and the names of some of the relationships on the left. Then complete the sentences below.

> grandmother grandfather granddaughter
> grandson mother father daughter son
> aunt uncle niece nephew cousin
> daughter-in-law son-in law sister-in-law
> brother-in-law

1 Sheila Simm is Henry Simm's daughter.
2 Edward Fowler is Henry Simm's son-in-law.
3 Walter Simm is Henry Simm's ....
4 Ann Dean is Henry Simm's ....
5 Maria Fowler is Walter Simm's niece.
6 John Simm is Sheila Simm's nephew.
7 Walter Simm is Maria Fowler's uncle.
8 Edward Fowler is Matthew Simm's ....
9 Maria Fowler is Ann Dean's ....
10 Ann Dean is Maria Fowler's ....
11 Ada Thomas is Elizabeth Fowler's grandmother.
12 Henry Simm is Elizabeth Fowler's ....
13 Elizabeth Fowler is Henry Simm's ....
14 Matthew Simm is Elizabeth Fowler's cousin.
15 Maria Fowler is John Simm's ....
16 Edward Fowler is Walter Simm's brother-in-law.
17 Ann Dean is Sheila Simm's ....

Compare your answers with a partner's.

b Draw your own family tree and give it to your partner. They can test you on the names of your relatives like this:

Example:
A: Who's Alfredo?
B: He's my cousin. *or*

A: What's your grandfather's name?
B: Pedro Sánchez.

18 People and relationships

Teacher's notes

Worksheet 2

Answers

1 a **This might be the order:**

1 You meet someone.
2 You get to know them.
3 You fall in love with them.
4 You get engaged.
5 You get married.
6 You get pregnant.
7 You have a baby.
8 You get divorced.

c
1 *false*
2 *true*
3 *true*
4 *false*
5 *false*
6 *true*
7 *true*
8 *true*

Tapescript

1 c **Listen to Paul talking about his marriage and follow the instructions on your worksheet.**

P: Well, I guess things started to go wrong just after we had Tom. We both knew it was going to be difficult but, well, it was the flat really; it just wasn't big enough for the three of us, so when he cried – he seemed to cry all the time – it disturbed us both during the day and kept both of us awake at night and we just couldn't get away from it and have any time to ourselves.
    Anyway, I started to lose my temper very quickly – you know, easily – not with the baby, I, I don't mean, no, I was very calm and patient when I was actually looking after him, but I used to lose my temper with Jane and we had terrible arguments and ...

W: Did they become physical fights?

P: No, no, no, no, nothing like that; I never touched Jane but I used to shout at her and smash things and – at first she shouted back at me, but after a while she responded by spending more and more time with Tom and she just ignored me. And when I saw her giving all her attention to him, I ... I suppose I was jealous of him and I felt very lonely.

W: And did you tell Jane about your feelings?

P: Well, I tried, once or twice, but there never seemed to be much time and when there was, we were both too tired. Anyway, er, in the end I left; I just couldn't stand it, and we finally got divorced last year.

W: And how do you feel about it now?

P: Well, I regret it, I regret it very much. But looking back on it, I think we were probably both too young. I mean, I don't think I was ready for the baby and things.

Key words and expressions

Verbs
hit
ignore
leave (someone)
regret
shout at

Adjectives
adventurous
cautious
(un)friendly
hard-working
intelligent
jealous
lazy
lonely
optimistic
(dis)organised
pessimistic
pregnant
self-confident
shy
stupid
(un)tidy

Other words and expressions
fall in love with someone
get divorced
get engaged
get married
get pregnant
get to know someone
have a baby
lose one's temper
meet someone

68

People and relationships 18

1 a What is the usual order for the following events? Number them 1–8 and then compare your order with your partner's.

You get married. ......
You fall in love with someone. ......
You get pregnant. ......
You get to know someone. ......
You get divorced. ......
You have a baby. ......
You meet someone. ......
You get engaged. ......

b Study the following sentences. Use a dictionary to find the meaning of any new words.

1 He ignored her. ......
2 He shouted at her. ......
3 He lost his temper. ......
4 He was jealous of her. ......
5 He hit her. ......
6 He felt lonely. ......
7 He left her. ......
8 He regrets what happened. ......

c ▭ Now listen to Paul talking about his marriage. Put *true* or *false* beside the sentences in **b**.

2 a Make sure you understand the words in the box. Use a dictionary to help you. Then use these words to complete the sentences below.

friendly unfriendly optimistic pessimistic
lazy hard-working stupid intelligent
shy self-confident organised disorganised
tidy untidy cautious adventurous

1 People who always wear a suit and tie are usually ....
2 People who never clean their shoes are usually ....
3 People who wear bright colours are usually ....
4 People who nearly always wear black clothes are usually ....
5 People who wear matching clothes are usually ....

b Compare and discuss your answers in groups.

1 a It is better to illustrate and develop these different word-building patterns on the board; you can then elicit examples from the class as you go along. When students carry out the activity, they should be encouraged to use dictionaries to check their answers.

Answers

1 a The words in brackets are not very common words in English.

predict	*invent*	*enjoy*	*imagine*	*adjust*	*adapt*
prediction	invention	enjoyment	imagination	adjustment	adaptation
(predictor)	inventor	enjoyable	imaginative	(adjuster)	adaptor
(predictive)	inventive		(imaginable)	adjustable	adaptable
predictable					

b Some possible answers are:

1   A belt, a strap.
2   'Gone with the Wind', 'A Room with a View'.
3   British weather, the result of a race/match.
4   The computer, seat belts, washing machine …
5   Human beings, the sparrow.
6   You will catch a cold next year.
7   A television.
8   The radio.
9   Chess.
10   Boxing, knitting, driving …

Key words and expressions

Nouns	Verbs, nouns and adjectives	Adjectives
actor	adapt – adaptable – adaptation – adaptor – unadaptable	affirmative
confusion	adjust – adjustable – adjuster – adjustment – unadjustable	attractive
education	enjoy – enjoyable – enjoyment – unenjoyable	convertible
improvement	imagine – imaginable – unimaginable – imagination –	readable
organisation	imaginative – unimaginative	sensitive
owner	invent – invention – inventive – inventor	
	predict – predictable – prediction – predictive – predictor –	
	unpredictable	

1 a We can make many nouns by adding suffixes in the following way:

Suffix	Example nouns
verb + -ment	improvement
-ion	education, confusion
-ation	organisation
-er/or	owner, actor

And we can make many adjectives like this:

Suffix	Example adjectives
verb + -ive	attractive
-ative/itive	affirmative, sensitive
-able/ible	readable, convertible

NB You will notice there is sometimes a change in spelling. One of the most common changes is to drop the final 'e'. For example:

sense – sensitive   organise – organisation

Study the verbs at the top of the table below. How many nouns and adjectives can you form from them using the suffixes above?

predict	invent	enjoy	imagine	adjust	adapt
....	....	....	....	....	....
....	....	....	....	....	....
....	....	....	....	....	....

b Work in groups of three. Can you think of an example for each of these?

1   Something you wear or part of something you carry which is adjustable.
2   A film which has been adapted from a book.
3   Something you can never predict accurately.
4   A recent invention which has had a great effect on your life.
5   An animal or insect which is very adaptable.
6   A prediction which will almost certainly come true.
7   A product which is adjustable but should not require adjustment.
8   An invention which helps some people to wake up and others to go to sleep.
9   A game which requires imagination but is often very predictable.
10   Something which one of you finds enjoyable and the others do not.

Answers

1 a useful
tactful
thoughtful
harmful

b 1 She's careless.
2 It's useless.
3 He's very thoughtless.
4 It's tasteless.
5 It was painless.
6 He's brainless.
7 It's harmless.
8 I'm very tactless.

2 a Suggested answers
1 Yes, they need to modernise it.
2 You can darken them.
3 No, they are going to strengthen it.
4 Yes, they need to economise.
5 You can lengthen them.
6 Do you think they will privatise it?
7 You can sharpen it with this.

b Other verbs that students might mention are:

blacken, deepen, frighten, harden, heighten, lighten, loosen, roughen, shorten, soften, tighten, straighten, thicken, whiten

centralise, computerise, criticise, industrialise, legalise, publicise, terrorise

Key words and expressions

Adjectives	Adjectives/nouns and verbs
brainless	dark – darken
endless	length – lengthen
homeless	sharp – sharpen
tasteless	strength – strengthen
toothless	wide – widen
careful – careless	economy – economise
harmful – harmless	modern – modernise
painful – painless	private – privatise
tactful – tactless	
thoughtful – thoughtless	

1 a The suffix '-less' often has the meaning 'without', e.g. a toothless man is a man without teeth. The opposite meaning is often conveyed with the suffix '-ful', e.g. *careless* and *careful* are opposites. (You must be careful, though. The opposite of *toothless* is <u>not</u> *toothful*.)

Which of the following adjectives can form an opposite with '-ful'?

useless   endless   tactless   thoughtless   homeless   harmless

b Try to think of a word with '-less' for the following sentences. You will need some words from the list in **a**, but others you will have to guess. Check in a dictionary to see if your word exists and has the correct meaning.

Example: These people have nowhere to live.   They're *homeless*..........................

1 She makes a lot of silly mistakes in her compositions.   She's ....
2 This tin opener doesn't work at all.   It's ....
3 He never thinks about other people.   He's very ....
4 This soup has no flavour at all.   It's ....
5 I had an injection but it didn't hurt.   It was ....
6 That boy is so stupid.   He's ....
7 Don't worry, the dog won't bite you.   It's ....
8 I'm always putting my foot in it.   I'm very ....

2 a We can form a number of verbs in English by adding '-en' or '-ize' (often '-*ise*' in British English) to an adjective or a noun:

sharp + en = sharpen (to make something sharper)
modern + ise = modernise (to make something modern)
economy + ise = economise (to make economies, be economical) (NB spelling change)

Respond to the sentences below. Form verbs by using the adjectives or nouns in the box + '-en' or '-ise', and use one in each reply.

| sharp   modern   wide   private   economy   strength   dark   length |

Example:

A: This road is too narrow and cars cannot overtake.
B: Yes, they need to widen it.

1 A: The town centre is looking terrible.
   B: ....
2 A: These photocopies are too light.
   B: ....
3 A: This bridge isn't strong enough for large lorries.
   B: ....
4 A: They are spending too much money.
   B: ....
5 A: These trousers are too short.
   B: ....
6 A: The transport system is run by the state.
   B: ....
7 A: This knife is blunt.
   B: ....

b Practise the dialogues with a partner. Can you think of any more verbs formed in these two ways?

Answers

1 a Allow students about ten minutes to complete the activity, and then if you have access to good monolingual dictionaries, tell them to look up the entries for *day* and *night* to see how many answers they can find.

day/night shift
one of these days
nightclub
day return
night watchman
daydream
last night
nightlife
goodnight/day
nightdress
overnight
the other day/night
the day before yesterday
the night before last

b

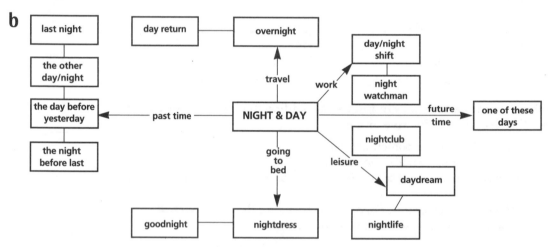

2 a One possible grouping is:

- insomnia   sleeping pills   go for a walk   count sheep   do exercises
- go to bed   fall asleep   have a nap   wake up   awake   get up
- dream   snore   have a nightmare   sleepwalk
- sleep like a log   have a restless night   be fast asleep

b Encourage students to follow up initial questions, i.e. if someone has a recurrent nightmare, try and find out what it is.

Key words and expressions

Nouns	Verb phrases	Time expressions	Other expressions
daydream	count sheep	last night	awake
day return	do exercises	overnight	fast asleep
insomnia	fall asleep	one of these days	
nightclub	go for a walk	the day before yesterday	
nightdress	go to bed	the night before last	
nightlife	have a nap	the other day	
night shift	have a nightmare	the other night	
night watchman	have a restless night		
sleeping pill	sleep like a log		
	sleepwalk		
	snore		

Night and day 20

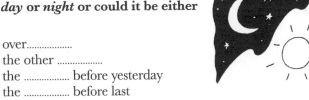

1 a There are a number of compound words or phrases containing *day* or *night*. Look at the lists below. Is the missing word *day* or *night* or could it be either of them?

.... shift   ....dream   over.................
one of these ....   last ....   the other ....
.................club   ....life   the .... before yesterday
.... return   good.................   the .... before last
.... watchman   ....dress

b Transfer the above words and phrases to this network.

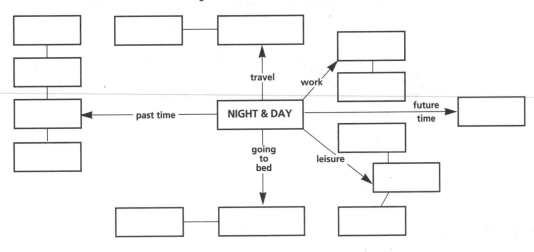

2 a Organise the following words and phrases into groups. You must decide what the groups are and how many groups there are. Work with a partner and compare your answers with another pair's when you have finished.

sleeping pills	fall asleep	go for a walk
dream	count sheep	go to bed
get up	wake up	insomnia
have a nightmare	sleepwalk	sleep like a log
do exercises	snore	have a restless night
be fast asleep	have a nap	awake

b Move round the class interviewing other students.

Find someone who ...	Name
... used to sleepwalk as a child.	_____
... has a recurrent nightmare.	_____
... does exercises either before they go to bed or immediately after they wake up.	_____
... finds it difficult to sleep in a strange bed.	_____
... can fall asleep easily when travelling on a coach, train or plane.	_____
... never takes sleeping pills.	_____
... enjoys having a nap during the day.	_____
... likes a hard bed.	_____
... suffers from insomnia.	_____
... snores a lot.	_____

 © Cambridge University Press 1996

Answers

1 a

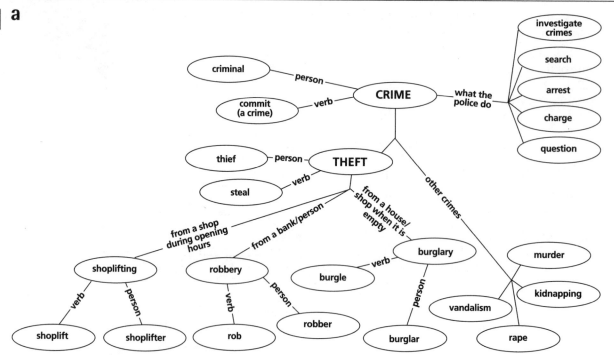

Key words and expressions

Nouns
prison sentence
victim

Verbs
arrest
be armed
charge
investigate
prevent
question
search
witness

Crime, person and verb
burglary – burglar – burgle
crime – criminal – commit (a crime)
kidnapping – kidnapper – kidnap
murder – murderer – murder
rape – rapist – rape
robbery – robber – rob
shoplifting – shoplifter – shoplift
theft – thief – steal
vandalism – vandal – vandalise

1 a Use a dictionary and your own knowledge to complete this vocabulary
network.

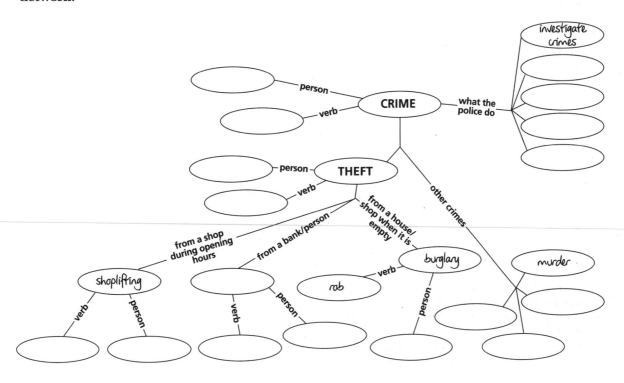

b Read through the questions and make sure you understand the words in
italics. Use a dictionary to help you.

1 Have you ever been the *victim* of a burglary or robbery? If so, what happened,
and how did you feel about it?

2 Have you ever *witnessed* a robbery, a burglary or shoplifting? If so, what
happened, and what action did you take?

3 Is the theft of car phones and car radios a common crime in your country? If so,
what action do people take to *prevent* it?

4 Do you believe that bank robbers should have longer *prison sentences* than burglars,
or are the two crimes very similar?

5 Are the police *armed* in your country? If so, do you think that is right, or would
you prefer to see policemen without guns?

6 Is there any crime which makes you particularly angry? Why?

Discuss the sentences in groups.

1 a You may have to preteach *average* and *arrest* (and *burgle* if students haven't done Worksheet 1).

Answers

a and b

1. False
2. True
3. True
4. True
5. False
6. True
7. True

c
1. alarm
2. locks
3. key
4. neighbours; police
5. light

Tapescript

2 b Listen to the advice on what to do if you wake up and hear a burglar in the house and follow the instructions on your worksheet.

- If you wake at night and hear someone in another room, or trying to break in, put all the lights on.
- Make a lot of noise by moving about.
- Do not go into the place where you can hear the noise.
- Phone the police from your bedroom, if possible.
- Find something you can use as a weapon if you are attacked – a comb or a bunch of keys.
- If you are on your own, call out loudly to an imaginary male companion: 'Tom, there's someone in the house.'
- Look out of the window after you hear the burglar leave.
- Note down what the burglar looks like, where he goes and the number of his car, if he has one.
- Call the police again.

Key words and expressions

Nouns	Verbs	Other words and expressions
burglar	burgle	late at night
burglar alarm	install	
burglary	protect	
lock		

Crime 21

1 a With a partner, discuss the following statements about burglaries in Britain. Do you think they are true or false?

1 The average burglary takes about 45 minutes.
2 Most burglars are young men.
3 Most burglars live quite near the houses they burgle.
4 Most burglaries happen when houses are empty.
5 Most burglaries take place late at night.
6 There is a 4% chance that you will be burgled this year.
7 Very few burglars are arrested.

b The text below gives information about burglaries in Britain. Read the text and compare the information with your answers to the questions in **a**.

PROFILE OF A BURGLARY

● The average burglary takes five minutes.

● Seven out of ten burglars are young men, living within a mile or two of your house and looking for easy opportunities.

● Most burglaries will occur in unoccupied houses through the back window in the afternoon and early evening.

● There is a chance in 25 that you will be burgled this year.

● Most burglaries result in a loss of under £100.

● Most burglars are never caught.

c How can you protect your house and prevent a burglary? Here are five things you can do. Complete each sentence with a suitable word and then write down three more ideas.

1 Install a burglar ....
2 Fit .... on all doors and windows.
3 Never leave the .... in the door or under the mat.
4 Tell your .... or the .... if you're going on holiday.
5 Leave the .... on when you go out.
6 ....
7 ....
8 ....

d When you have finished, discuss the ideas in groups. Which are the most effective and which are the least effective?

2 a What would you do if you woke in the night and heard a burglar in the house? Discuss your ideas in groups and make a list of possible actions.

b 🔲 Now listen to some instructions on what to do if you hear a burglar in your house. Make notes. Are any of the points the same as those on your list? If there are any different ones, do you agree with them?

Answers

1 a

Synonyms	
jumper	pullover
wait a minute	hang on
rude	impolite
wealthy	rich
healthy	fit
nervous	tense

Opposites	
optimistic	pessimistic
laugh	cry
dirty	clean
cruel	kind
thin	fat
ugly	good-looking

b Other possible synonyms and opposites are:

Synonyms	
jumper	sweater
wait a minute	hold on
optimistic	positive
pessimistic	negative
fat	overweight
thin	skinny
ugly	unattractive
good-looking	attractive

Opposites	
rude	polite
rich	poor
healthy	unhealthy/ill
fit	unfit
nervous/tense	calm/relaxed
clean	unclean
kind	unkind
ugly	beautiful

(**No possible synonyms for** *laugh* **and** *cry*.)

c 1 jumper/pullover
2 wait a minute / hang on
3 nervous/tense
4 laugh
5–8 *open answers*

Key words and expressions

Nouns	Verbs	Adjectives		Other words and expressions
jumper	cry	alive	marvellous	hang on
pullover	laugh	clean	nervous	wait a minute
		cruel	optimistic	
		dead	pessimistic	
		dirty	rich	
		fat	rude	
		fit	tense	
		good-looking	thin	
		healthy	ugly	
		impolite	wealthy	
		kind	wonderful	

1 a A useful way to learn new vocabulary is to organise it into pairs/groups of synonyms or opposites. For example:

wonderful and marvellous (synonyms)
dead and alive (opposites)

Find six pairs of synonyms and six pairs of opposites in the box, and complete the table below. Use a dictionary to help you.

jumper	laugh	rich	fat
wait a minute	impolite	clean	cry
optimistic	dirty	tense	ugly
rude	healthy	cruel	hang on
pullover	fit	pessimistic	kind
wealthy	nervous	thin	good-looking

Synonyms		*Opposites*	
....	....	....	....
....	....	....	....
....	....	....	....
....	....	....	....
....	....	....	....
....	....	....	....

b Look at each pair of words again. Can you find another synonym or opposite for either word? Use a dictionary to help you, then compare your answers in groups.

c From the words in **a** and **b**, write down something that ...

1 ... you wear. ....
2 ... you may say to someone in a hurry. ....
3 ... you may be before an important exam. ....
4 ... you like to do. ....
5 ... you think you are. ....
6 ... you don't think you are. ....
7 ... you would like to be in the future. ....
8 ... you were in the past. ....

Discuss your answers in groups.

Clarissa was attracted to Dave because he was so different from anyone she had ever met.

Answers

1 a The numbers here relate to **d**. The near synonyms are:

holiday travellers – holidaymakers
delays – hold-ups   2
dispute – row   1, 2
failure – breakdown   1, 4
chaos – confusion
unable to leave – stranded at   2

b When students have completed the activity and you have checked their answers, it is important to point out that textual synonymy is not always a matter of two words which are almost identical in meaning – often the two words will only act as synonyms in one particular context. Students must be prepared for the fact that the contextual meaning is not always identical to a dictionary definition of a word's meaning.

(The numbers here relate to **d**.)

colleagues – friends   1, 2, 3, 4
bumped into – met   2, 4
liver – meat   1, 4
surprising – a bit of a shock   2
because – as   4
said – told me   4, 5

it turned out that – apparently   4
scared – frightened
shop – butcher's 1
dog – animal   1
shy – embarrassed   4

finance – money   1, 3
wealthy – well-off
problem – trouble   4
disgusting – revolting
kids – children   2

c This final activity redresses the balance, and it may also reassure you if you were worried about sending your students away with the idea that *shy* and *embarrassed* mean the same thing.

d The answers are in **a** and **b** above. (If there is no number, it means they are almost the same in meaning and the types do not apply.)

Key words and expressions

Nouns	Verbs	Adjectives	Opinion markers	Other words and expressions
armchair	bump into	disgusting	apparently	bit of a shock
breakdown	hold up	embarrassed	it turned out that	had a bad day
chaos		frightened		strict vegetarian
colleague		ghastly		
confusion		revolting		
delay		scared of		
dispute		shy		
failure		stranded		
finance		surprising		
guy		terrible		
holidaymaker		wealthy		
kid		well-off		
liver				
trouble				

Synonyms and opposites 22

1 a We often repeat information in a text using different vocabulary. Find synonyms in this text for the underlined words.

<u>Holiday travellers</u> faced long <u>delays</u> today after a French air traffic control <u>dispute</u> and a double computer <u>failure</u> threw Europe's airways into <u>chaos</u>.	A number of flights were held up for more than six hours and one group of holidaymakers was <u>unable to leave</u> Portugal today, as scheduled. So far, they have been stranded at Faro Airport for more than 20 hours.	A row over working conditions is responsible for the problems with the French air traffic control and the resulting hold-ups, but the confusion has been made worse by the simultaneous breakdown of important computers at Brest and Prestwick.

b Find synonyms in the box for the underlined words in the text.

> well-off   meat   a bit of a shock   money   as   trouble
> butcher's   told me   embarrassed   revolting   met
> frightened   apparently   children   friends   animal

I bumped into an old colleague of mine yesterday. His name is Oliver Knight, but he was always known as 'OK' to his <u>colleagues</u>. I <u>bumped into</u> him buying liver in a shop down the road. Now this was surprising because OK is a strict vegetarian and has always felt that <u>liver</u> is disgusting. 'It's for the kids,' he said by way of explanation.

This too was <u>surprising</u> <u>because</u> OK had always been a bachelor and certainly hadn't had time to become a father since I last saw him. 'They're my wife's from a previous marriage,' he <u>said</u> shyly.

It turned out that he had married someone called Petra, and she had come complete with a family – a boy and a girl, and a dog. I knew that OK was scared of dogs, so I asked him how he managed. <u>It turned out that</u> he had been <u>scared</u> at first, but now they were the best of friends; in fact, the huge dog I had seen waiting outside the <u>shop</u> was the <u>dog</u> in question.

'It must have affected your finances, taking on a family,' I said. You see, OK wasn't a wealthy man.

He looked a little <u>shy</u> for a moment. '<u>Finance</u> isn't a problem. Petra's rather <u>wealthy</u>, you see, and she's got a very good job,' he said. 'The <u>problem</u> is that I stay at home and have to cook all this <u>disgusting</u> meat for the <u>kids</u>.'

c Two words may act as synonyms in one text, but that does not mean they are exactly the same. There are many possible differences:

1 One word is more general than the other, e.g. *seat* is more general than *armchair*.
2 One word is more formal or colloquial than the other, e.g. *guy* is more colloquial than *man*.
3 One word is more common than the other, e.g. *terrible* is more common than *ghastly*.
4 The meaning may be similar in one context but not in another, e.g. you can say *a busy shop* and *a crowded shop*. You can say *a busy day at work* but not *a crowded day at work*.
5 The words have the same meaning, but different grammar, e.g. *Can I borrow your pen?*, but *Can you lend me your pen?*

d Find examples of 1–5 in Parts **a** and **b** above.

Answers

1 a **The activities are:**

skiing, water skiing, climbing, volleyball, hiking (walking), windsurfing, squash, camping, sailing, weight training, riding, scuba diving (skin diving), jogging, basketball.

Key words

Sports	Other nouns
basketball	skill
camping	stamina
climbing	strength
hiking (walking)	
jogging	
riding	
sailing	
skiing	
scuba diving (skin diving)	
squash	
volleyball	
water skiing	
weight training	
windsurfing	

1 a Look at the pictures. What activities can you see ? Use a dictionary or ask
other students if you don't know the answers. Then try and find a person in
the class who enjoys each of the activities. You can ask questions like this:

A: Do you ever go (skiing)? *or*
   Do you ever do any (skiing)? *or*
   Do you ever play (volleyball)?
B: Yes, sometimes.
A: Do you enjoy it?

b What abilities do you need for these sports and activities? In groups, discuss
and then complete the following chart like this:

✓✓✓ = You need a lot of strength/skill/stamina.
  ✓✓ = You need quite a lot of strength/skill/stamina.
   ✓ = You don't need much strength/skill/stamina.
   ✗ = You don't need any strength/skill/stamina.

Activity	Strength	Skill	Stamina
Jogging	✓	✗	✓✓

Answers

2 a and b These are some possible answers. The answers from the cassette are underlined:

1 meet people / make friends
2 fun
3 keep fit
4 competing
5 relaxing/satisfying/enjoyable
6 exciting/exhilarating

Tapescript

2 b Listen and follow the instructions on your worksheet.

1
M: Well, I haven't really got any hobbies, but, er I've only recently moved to this area, so I decided to join this bridge club because I thought it might be a good way to meet people. To tell you the truth, I haven't really made many friends, but I do enjoy bridge – very much – so it's been quite good for me.

2
W: I play quite a lot of badminton actually, just for fun - I don't believe in taking sport too seriously. You know, some people get very aggressive when they play team games. I hate that.

3
W: I suppose my main relaxation is aerobics – if you can call it relaxation. I do it twice a week, mostly to keep fit, because I'm in a desk job and I really don't get that much exercise unless I force myself to do something energetic.

4
M: Well, I play a lot of football in the winter, mostly for pleasure – nothing serious. But my main sport is athletics and I think the thing I like about it is, er well, I, I enjoy competing against other people, and er, oh, I get a lot of satisfaction when I win!

5
M: I spend most of my free time in the garden. There always seems to be something that needs doing, but I don't mind: I enjoy it. I find it very relaxing and very satisfying.

6
W: My latest craze is hang gliding, and the thing I love about it is that it's so exciting. You just can't imagine, unless you actually do it, what it's like to just float in space hundreds of feet up. It's fabulous.

Key words and expressions

Sports and leisure activities	Other nouns	Adjectives	Verbs	Other words and expressions
aerobics	jazz	active	compete	do aerobics
athletics	machine operator	bored		do something for (fun)
badminton	musical instrument	creative		do something for (pleasure)
bridge	pharmacist	exciting		go to a class in (photography)
chess	team	monotonous		join (a club)
'do-it-yourself' ('D.I.Y.')	workaholic	relaxing		keep fit
flower arranging		satisfying		make friends
flying		stimulating		take up (photography)
gardening		stressful		
hang gliding		tiring		
jogging		unemployed		
squash		worried		
yoga				

1 a Read the texts and then choose the best hobby for each of these people from the box. Work in groups and use a dictionary where necessary.

Susan is a pharmacist and spends most of her day working alone. She has several hobbies – she makes her own clothes and enjoys gardening – but she would like to get out of the house and meet people.

Mary used to be a teacher, but she has been unemployed for almost a year. She spends most of her day reading but is now getting very bored. She is also very worried abut her future.

John has a very stressful job in an advertising agency. His friends think he is a workaholic and he does not have much time for hobbies. However, he would like to find a hobby which is both stimulating and relaxing.

Brian is a machine operator. His job is tiring but very monotonous. He spends most of his spare time watching his local football team and listening to jazz, but he would like an active, creative hobby which would give him more personal satisfaction.

> learn to play a musical instrument   join a chess club
> take up photography   take up 'do-it-yourself' ('D.I.Y.')   take up squash
> take up yoga   go to an evening class in flower arranging   go jogging
> take flying lessons

b Can you think of one more hobby (not in the box) for each of these people?

2 a Complete the following sentences with a suitable word or phrase.

Speaker 1:   I joined a bridge club because it's a good way to ....
Speaker 2:   I play badminton just for ....
Speaker 3:   I do aerobics mostly to ....
Speaker 4:   I do athletics mostly because I enjoy .... against other people.
Speaker 5:   I do a lot of gardening and I find it very ....
Speaker 6:   The thing I love about hang gliding is that it's so ....

b 🔲 Now listen to what the six people above actually say, and write down their answers (if they are different from yours).

c Think of your favourite sport or leisure activity. Why do you do it? In groups, discuss what other people do and why they do it.

Answers

1 a

1	'Thanks very much.'	'Not at all.'
2	'Anything else?'	'No, that's all, thanks.'
3	'Can I help you?'	'I'm being served, thanks.'
4	'I'm sorry I'm late.'	'Never mind, don't worry.'
5	'What's the matter?'	'Nothing. Why?'
6	'How long does it take?'	'About twenty minutes.'
7	'Have a nice weekend.'	'Yes, you too.'
8	'Could I leave a message?'	'Yes, of course, I'll just get a pen.'
9	'Have you got a light?'	'Sorry, I don't smoke.'
10	'Could I borrow your pen?'	'Yes, help yourself.'
11	'Have you got the time?'	'Yes. Quarter to seven.'
12	'Do you mind if I open the window?'	'No, go ahead.'

C Here are some possible answers:

1 'Have a good day.'
2 'Anything else?'
3 'Have you got the time?' / 'What's the time?'
4 'Could/Can I have a biscuit? / borrow this cassette?'
5 'What's the matter?'
6 'Can I help you?'
7 'How long does it take?'
8 'Could/Can I leave a message?'
9 'Have you got a light?'
10 'Thanks very much.' / 'Thanks a lot.'
11 'Do you mind if I shut the door?'
12 'I'm sorry I'm late.' / 'I'm sorry I forgot to phone you.'

Key words and expressions

Questions	Replies
Anything else?	No, that's all, thanks.
Can I help you?	Yes, please. / I'm being served, thanks.
Could I leave a message?	Yes, of course. / Sure.
Do you mind if I (do something)?	No, go ahead.
Have you got a light?	Yes. / Sorry, I don't smoke.
Have you got the time?	Yes. (Quarter to seven.)
How long does it take?	(About twenty minutes.)
What's the matter?	Nothing. Why?

Statements	Replies
Have a nice weekend.	Yes, you too.
I'm sorry I'm late.	Never mind, don't worry.
Thanks very much.	Not at all.

1 a Choose a suitable reply from B for each of the statements or
questions from A.

A says …

B replies …

1	Thanks very much.	Yes, help yourself.
2	Anything else?	Never mind, don't worry.
3	Can I help you?	About twenty minutes.
4	I'm sorry I'm late.	I'm being served, thanks.
5	What's the matter?	No, go ahead.
6	How long does it take?	Yes. Quarter to seven.
7	Have a nice weekend.	Sorry, I don't smoke.
8	Could I leave a message?	Not at all.
9	Have you got a light?	Yes, you too.
10	Could I borrow your pen?	No, that's all, thanks.
11	Have you got the time?	Nothing. Why?
12	Do you mind if I open the window?	Yes, of course, I'll just get a pen.

b Practise the exchanges with a partner. Make sure you can say the
expressions clearly and without hesitation.

c Now cover up **a** above and write suitable statements or questions that would
produce these replies from B.

Example:
A: 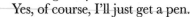 Thanks very much. .... B: Not at all.

1 A: .... B: Yes, you too.

2 A: .... B: No, that's all, thanks.

3 A: .... B: Half past six.

4 A: .... B: Yes, help yourself.

5 A: .... B: Nothing. Why?

6 A: .... B: I'm being served, thanks.

7 A: .... B: About half an hour on the bus.

8 A: .... B: Sure, I'll just get a pen.

9 A: .... B: Sorry, I don't smoke.

10 A: .... B: Not at all.

11 A: .... B: No, go ahead.

12 A: .... B: Never mind, don't worry.

d Check your answers with **a**.

e Practise the different questions and statements and see if your partner can
give you logical replies in each case. (Sometimes these will be the same as
the answers above, but sometimes there may be many possible answers.)